W9-BXH-311

THE ABSOLUTELY ESSENTIAL®
GUIDE TO
ORLANDO

Where the World Goes on Vacation

O 87   ORLANDO. FLORIDA. THE CITY BEAUTIFUL

ROSE GARDEN ON LAKE EOLA

2763-30

THE ABSOLUTELY ESSENTIAL® COMPANY
WINTER PARK, FLORIDA
OCTOBER 2003

Other Books by
THE ABSOLUTELY ESSENTIAL® COMPANY:

THE ABSOLUTELY ESSENTIAL® GUIDE TO WINTER PARK

HAND-COLORED
POST CARD

THE ABSOLUTELY ESSENTIAL® COMPANY
Post Office Box 1492
Winter Park, Florida 32790-1492

rchaps@msn.com

Photographed and Published by Siewert.

THIS SPACE FOR MESSAGE.   THIS SPACE FOR ADDRESS.

© 2003 by Robin Chapman
Library of Congress Control Number: 2003090452
ISBN 0-9714156-1-7

October 2003

THE ABSOLUTELY ESSENTIAL®
GUIDE TO
ORLANDO

Where the World Goes on Vacation

BY
ROBIN CHAPMAN

O-22—Hedge of Flame Vine and Spanish Type Home, Orlando, Fla., "The City Beautiful"

Illustrated with a collection of vintage postcards

WIGWAM VILLAGE No. 4

ORANGE BLOSSOM TRAIL, U. S. 441 AND U. S. 17; U. S. 92

ONIAL SWIMMING POOL — COLONIAL ORANGE COURT HOTEL — ORLANDO, FLORIDA

St. Charles Hotel, Orlando, Fla.

To Evelyn W. Pettit:
editor and friend

ORLANDO →

**WELCOME
TO THE
CITY BEAUTIFUL**

CONTENTS

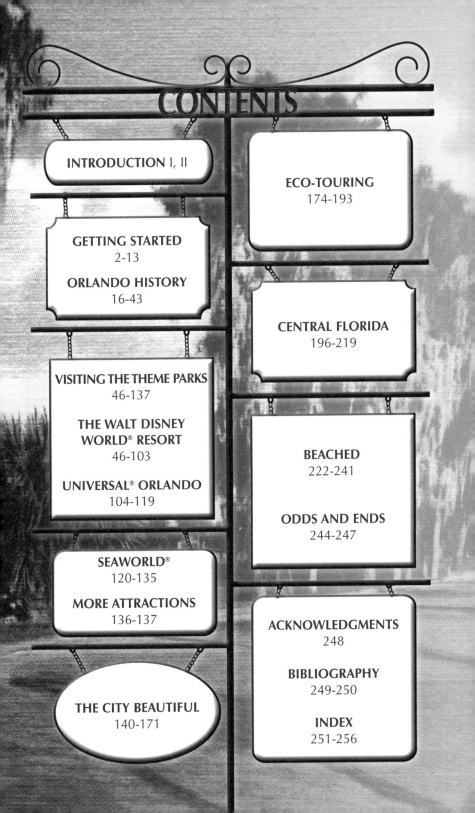

A Foreword
VINTAGE POSTCARDS

Orange Avenue looking North, Orlando, Fla.

Orlando, looking like a set from an old movie, in this vintage postcard.
Courtesy of the Florida State Archives.

This is my second guidebook illustrated with vintage Florida postcards. I would love to take credit for this idea, but the truth is: I just happened to stumble over it. I was working on my first book, *The Absolutely Essential® Guide to Winter Park*, and wondering how to illustrate it when a friend suggested I speak with a local man, Rick Frazee, who had a collection of Winter Park postcards. I was busy, and I filed the idea away. Then I happened to meet Rick, who told me his collection included more than 800 postcards of Winter Park. Good grief, I thought: who knew there would be so many postcards of such a small town? Still, to be polite, I said I would be happy to look at them. The minute I opened the binders of his collection, I was wowed. The lovely, hand-colored cards, their textures, their traditional Florida themes—even the messages on the backs, and the stamps—were beautiful and interesting. They were just what I had been looking for. These cards provide us with a graphic record of Florida tourism: from its beginnings in the 19th century to the present day. I am pleased, once again, to be able to share that record with you, this time in *The Absolutely Essential® Guide to Orlando*. My thanks to the many people and agencies who allowed me to use their collections. And to Rick Frazee, whose collection was, for me, the beginning of a wonderful new adventure.

WELCOME TO ORLANDO

I came to Central Florida to take a job in television news. I had spent all my adult life working in newsrooms around the country, and I took pride in being able to learn quickly about any new region or assignment. Still, the first day I sat down to anchor the news in Orlando, I didn't know DeLand from DeBary, nor Palm Bay from Palm Beach. I was lucky that the viewers were tolerant of my learning curve. It didn't take long for me to be struck by the beauty of this place: the beaches were more beautiful, the environment more exotic, the sunsets more dramatic, the skies brighter than anywhere else I'd ever lived. Being an incurable romantic, I thought I might fall in love in Orlando. What I didn't expect, was that I would fall in love *with* Orlando.

When I left television, I took a job working as a creative executive for the Walt Disney World Company. Disney is one of the biggest companies in the world, and I'm not going to tell you it was an easy transition. I tried to do what any good journalist would do when plopped down in an unfamiliar situation: I kept my eyes and ears open and took notes. At Disney I met the other Orlando—the Orlando of tourism and international travel. Working beside some of the toughest and smartest people I'd ever met, I learned why the business of tourism works so well in this pretty place. In *The Absolutely Essential® Guide to Orlando*, I'll share with you some of what I learned during five years inside Disney, and introduce you to the other things I've grown to love about this region. I hope, as you read along, the smell of citrus blossoms and the warmth of the sun will shine through these pages and lead you directly to our door.

This vintage postcard, dated about 1906, is even more fun than the usual vintage card because it calls Orlando's best-known park "Lake Cola."

O-94 Fountain in Lake Eola Park, Orlando, Fla.
"The City Beautiful"

O.40. ORLANDO, FLORIDA, THE CITY B

1043

A VIEW OF THE CITY, LOOKING ACROSS LAKE EOLA.

BEAUTIFUL

GETTING STARTED

Florida   0-19

"The City Beautif...

ORLANDO, FLORIDA, THE CITY BEAUTIFUL.   0.49

BAND STAND ON LAKE EOLA.

105197

Getting Started

FLORIDA STATE CAPITOL IN TALLAHASSEE

FLORIDA STATE FLAG

FLORIDA STATE BIRD MOCKING BIRD

"WAY DOWN UPON THE SWANEE RIBBER"   FLORIDA'S STATE SONG

FLORIDA STATE FLOWER THE ORANGE BLOSSOM

Orientation

HI, Y'ALL!

Y ou arrive on a pressurized jet, get into an air-conditioned vehicle, check into a climate-controlled room on a street filled with hotels, motels, restaurants, and T-shirt shops. Sometimes it seems as if Orlando exists in isolation, like Fantasy Island.

WHERE AM I? The truth is that when you're in Orlando, you're right in the middle of the State of Florida, the southern-most state in the United States. Since you are here, you might find it interesting to learn a little bit about this part of the world.

DEEP IN THE HEART OF DIXIE Florida became the 27th state in the United States on March 3, 1845. In 1861, Florida voted to secede from the Union with the rest of the South, though 2,000 men from the state enlisted to fight for the North. Florida made it through the Civil War relatively unscathed. In fact, Florida had so little development back then that the ferocious Union General William Tecumseh Sherman ("War is hell!") didn't even bother coming here to burn anything down.

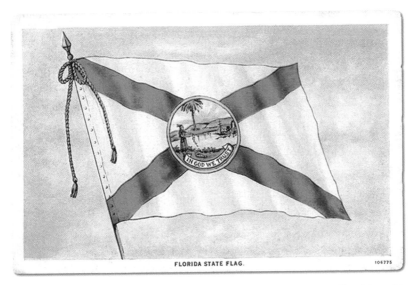

FLORIDA STATE FLAG.   106775

DARLING, I (DON'T) SURRENDER Florida's state flag was originally plain white with just the state seal in the center. But that changed in the 1890s when Florida's legislators figured this practically-all-white flag looked a little too much like a flag of surrender. The red cross in the field of white was thus added.

AND WE SMELL GREAT TOO! The Florida state flower, so named in 1909, isn't really a flower at all, at least not in the traditional sense. It is the orange blossom—a beautiful reminder of one of Florida's biggest industries.

Florida Orange Blossom Time

PHOTO COURTESY FLORIDA CYPRESS GARDENS

AND IF THAT MOCKINGBIRD DON'T SING? We have some beautiful exotic birds here in Florida's subtropical environment—egrets, ibises, herons, and anhingas, to name just a few. But wouldn't you know it? The Florida state bird is the common mockingbird, *Mimus polyglottos*. This talkative imitator does spend all year in Florida, but we nevertheless have to share him: the mockingbird is also the state bird of Arkansas, Mississippi, Tennessee, and Texas.

HE'D RATHER HAVE BEEN IN PITTSBURGH Florida's state song is "Old Folks at Home" written by Stephen Foster (1826-1864) in 1851 and often remembered by its first line, "Way down upon the Swanee River." The river in north Florida is actually the *Suwannee*, though it is pronounced as Foster spelled it. He never actually saw the river himself. He spent most of his life in Pittsburgh.

Chorus
Way down upon the Swanee River
Far, far away
That's where my heart is yearning ever,
That's where the old folks stay.

Florida's demographics actually do match the song's title: more than half the state's population (55.3%) is 51 years of age or older. Perhaps because of that, we are not often inclined to use the term "old folks" here in Florida except, of course, when singing Mr. Foster's lovely song.

Excuse us while we play a little shuffleboard and relax under our jacarandas.
Postcards courtesy of the Orange County Regional History Center.

Quo Vadis?

BY ORLANDO YOU MEAN ... ?

The State of Florida has much more definite boundaries than does the place we call Orlando. What "Orlando" is, depends upon your definition.

THE CITY OF ORLANDO This is a relatively small place, with a population of about 186,000.

> **METRO ORLANDO** If you include all the surrounding counties to which, for example, local television stations broadcast their news, you have a large metropolitan area indeed. Metro Orlando is one of the top 20 metro areas in the United States, with a population of 1.6 million.

DESTINATION ORLANDO This is the place to which 40 million visitors come each year. Quite a few of them spend almost no time at all within the city limits but feel quite certain when they go home that they have returned from Orlando. Not that there's anything wrong with that.

CENTRAL FLORIDA You could call it a slice of real estate in the middle of Florida. And if you said that, you could also call Orlando its capital.

All these Orlandos make up the Orlando that visitors come to see. From city to county to region to destination—this is a place designed to make people feel welcome, and to show everyone who comes here a very good time.

S-160 SUNSHINE AND SHADOWS, A RESIDENTIAL STREET IN FLORIDA

Water Hyacinths in Florida

NAMES AND PLACES

Here are the origins of a few of the words you hear frequently in Florida:

Mosquito: The Spaniards gave this pesky little bug its name. A *mosca* is a fly in Spanish, and *ito* means "little."

Florida: In his book *Florida Place Names*, Allen Morris calls this the first name Europeans brought to this continent. It is attributed to Juan Ponce de Leon, who first set eyes on this new land Easter Sunday, 1513. It was a pretty, flowery-looking place (they hadn't yet met our mosquitos), so the land became *La Florida*, "The Flower Place."

Osceola: The name of the Seminoles' celebrated warrior is derived from the Creek word or sound *os-cin-ye-hula* believed to be a sort of a cry the Indians made when they drank their ceremonial black drink made from yaupon leaves. When young Indian leader Billy Powell took the name "Osceola," he thus became "black drink man."

Kissimmee: This one is a mystery. Experts at the Smithsonian Institution say this is definitely an Indian name, and the Seminoles agree, but even they do not know its meaning. The name is believed to have come from the Ais Caloosas Indians, who were wiped out in the 16th century.

Alligator: Another American creature named by the Spanish, though the word was corrupted by English speakers. The Spaniards called it *el lagarto* or "the lizard," and that, somehow became alligator.

O.37—Orlando Municipal Airport
Orlando, Fla.
"The City Beautiful"

Ah, the days when airport transit was easier and less stressful. This vision of Orlando International Airport courtesy of the Orange County Regional History Center.

Going My Way?

TRAINS AND BOATS AND PLANES

Here are some of your Orlando transit options:

Orlando International Airport (MCO): The busiest airport in the region is **Orlando International**, known by the initials **MCO** because it began life long ago as McCoy Field. More than 26 million people travel through MCO each year on 55 different airlines. It is now the 24th-busiest airport in the world, just a few passengers per year behind New York's JFK. It is easy to use, with a monorail that saves your feet as it transports you to and from the gates. International travelers who deplane here spend an average of 46 minutes moving through customs, immigration, and baggage pick-up. If you rent a car, you will notice as you depart that exits on the roadway to all the attractions are very well marked. Shuttles, taxis, etc. are available. *Operated by the Greater Orlando Aviation Authority, which also operates Orlando Executive Airport, One Airport Boulevard, Orlando, Florida 32827-4399.* www.orlandoairports.net   **407-825-2001**

Orlando Sanford International Airport (SFB): Slightly more than a million people use this airport each year, and most of these travel on international charters. SFB is just 18 miles northeast of the City of Orlando, so it can be a convenient choice. *Operated by the Sanford Airport Authority, One Red Cleveland Boulevard, Sanford, Florida 32773*
www.orlandosanfordairport.com   **407-585-4000**

Melbourne International Airport (MLB): Smaller than SFB, this airport is about an hour southeast of MCO and handles 600,000 passengers annually. Though it is not served by the range of airlines that serve MCO, it is just 25 miles south of Port Canaveral, which makes it the closest airport to the cruise terminals and the Space Coast. *Operated by the Melbourne Airport Authority, One Air Terminal Parkway, Melbourne, Florida 32901-1888*
www.mlbair.com   **321-723-6227**

Daytona Beach International Airport (DAB): This airport went international in 1992, and it now handles about 500,000 travelers each year. It is quite a distance from Orlando: 55 miles from the city and 75 miles from Walt Disney World. But, if you look at it another way, it is only three-quarters of a mile from the Daytona International Speedway! *Operated by Volusia County, 700 Catalina Drive, Daytona Beach, Florida 32114*
www.flydaytonafirst.com   **386-248-8069**

S. S. Florida

Port Canaveral began by serving cargo ships in 1955, and it is now the busiest cruise port in the Western Hemisphere, with service (at last count) from at least nine cruise lines, including the Disney Cruise Line. The port is 45 miles east of Orlando International Airport, an easy ride on S.R. 528, which has the best nickname for a road in the state: the Bee Line Expressway. Who wouldn't want to zoom along on that? (To help you keep your heading, there is even a little bee on each Bee Line Expressway sign.)

www.portcanaveral.org   **888-PortCan (888-767-8226)**

O.68.   ORLANDO, FLORIDA, THE CITY BEAUTIFUL.

NEW A.C.L.R.R. STATION.   110298

Amtrak provides national passenger service in the United States, and the line serves all major Central Florida cities including Sanford, Winter Park, Orlando, and Kissimmee. **Coach USA** meets every train that comes into the Orlando station, with shuttles to all the area hotels and attractions. If you want to make arrangements in advance, call Coach USA at **407-826-9999**. Amtrak schedules and reservations are available on the Web, or at Amtrak's toll-free number.

www.amtrak.com   **800-872-7245**

THE "A" TRAIN

Central Florida is one of just two places in the United States where you can catch the Auto Train. It runs daily between Lorton, Virginia, just outside of Washington, DC, and Sanford, Florida, just 20 minutes north of Orlando. If you are in the Northeastern United States and you want to bring your vehicle with you to Florida, but you hate the thought of that long drive, the Auto Train has the best solution going. Drive to Lorton, where Amtrak will put your vehicle right on the train while you settle into a little roomette or a comfortable seat in coach. The train leaves Lorton in the late afternoon and arrives in Central Florida the next morning, just after breakfast. Dinner and breakfast are included in the ticket price, and there is something almost old-fashioned about the service. If you get a roomette, your porter will make up your bed while you are having your dinner. The train—which Amtrak says is the longest in the world—leaves once daily both northbound and southbound. You can ride the train only with your vehicle, but everything from an RV to a motorcycle qualifies. The Auto Train carries about a quarter of a million passengers each year, which makes it one of the few routes on which Amtrak makes a profit. I suppose train rides are not for everyone these days, but I've ridden the Auto Train a number of times and I highly recommend it. *For more information on Amtrak and the Auto Train, phone* **800-872-7245***, or log on to* www.amtrak.com.

OK, this isn't the Auto Train, but this is how I imagine it looks!
The Atlantic Coast Line Streamliner ran direct summer service from Orlando
to Washington, DC, and New York City, beginning May 14, 1941.

The new Expressway leading through Downtown Orlando, Florida

This is I-4 shortly after it was constructed. Sorry to tell you it hasn't had so few cars on it since. Postcard courtesy of the Florida State Archives.

Coping

MOTORING MADNESS

If you do any driving in Central Florida, you will have to gather up your courage and face Interstate 4, also known as I-4. It is the main artery between Daytona Beach and Tampa, and it is the most direct route through Orlando. The road was built between 1960 and 1962, when the entire population of the State of Florida was under 5 million. Forty years later, with the Florida population approaching 17 million, I-4, which once routed 16,000 cars a day through Orlando, must now handle 10 times that many. During the first part of the 21st century, the Florida Department of Transportation has been widening I-4 to three lanes, plus a high occupancy vehicle (HOV) lane, in each direction. When this is completed, all buses, emergency vehicles, and other vehicles with two or more occupants will be able to use the HOV lanes, which will (presumably) be somewhat less crowded than the others. Still and all: the best bet on I-4 is to avoid peak traffic times (7:00-9:00 a.m. and 3:00-6:00 p.m.). If you head onto the interstate just ten minutes *before* 7:00 a.m., for example, it can often save you much more than ten minutes driving time. Be forewarned: a bad accident can close I-4. Tune in to traffic reports on television before you head out, and listen for updates on your car radio. I-4 is not a bad road. But it is at its best when you're on the off-ramp and it is in your rear view mirror.

WEATHER

During eight months of each year, from October through May, the weather in Orlando is fabulous. The four months from June through September are hot. During those months, you can expect high humidity and frequent afternoon thunderstorms. If you use your head—placing a sun hat on it, for example; sheltering it when need be under an umbrella; and getting it the heck inside when you spot lightning—the summer can be very pleasant. There is almost always a soft breeze. During the mornings and evenings, the air surrounds you like a caress. Unless you are sensitive to the chill of air-conditioning, you won't need to carry a wrap. During an Orlando summer, it isn't possible to spend too much time in a swimming pool. Napping on the veranda is also highly recommended.

Average Temperature

	High		Low	
January	71°F	21°C	49°F	9.4°C
February	73	22	50	10
March	78	25	55	12
April	83	28	59	15
May	88	31	66	19
June	91	32	72	22
July	92	33	73	23
August	92	33	73	23
September	90	32	72	22
October	85	29	66	19
November	79	26	58	14
December	73	21	51	10

Average Rainfall

	Inches	Centimeters
January	2.2	5.5
February	3.0	7.6
March	3.2	8.1
April	1.8	4.5
May	3.6	9.1
June	7.3	18.5
July	7.3	18.5
August	6.8	17.2
September	6.0	15.2
October	2.4	6.0
November	2.3	5.8
December	2.2	5.5

Gary's Duck Inn
South Orange Blossom Trail
ORLANDO, FLORIDA

JUMBO SHRIMP P

GARY'S
LIQUORS

O-6—Entrance to Orlando Air Base, Orlando, Fla.

RLANDO, FLORIDA,

ORLANDO AIR BASE

RESTAURANT
POSTAL
TELEGRAPH

9755

ANDO, FLA.

ORLANDO HISTORY

Midwinter at Orlando, Florida.

...NGE GROVE, ORLANDO, FLO...

ORLANDO HISTORY

A NATIONAL AIRLINER
OVER THE FLORIDA EVERGLADES

The days of future past in a vintage postcard courtesy of the Florida State Archives.

The Florida Seminoles

THE UNTAMED TRIBE

The only written records we have of the native Americans who were in Florida before the Spanish arrived in 1513, are from the Spanish themselves. From the archaeological record, scientists believe the loose configuration of Timucuan tribes who populated Central Florida had been on the peninsula for thousands of years before the arrival of the Europeans. The Timucua were a peaceful people who lived in primitive settlements and—in a bow to the climate of the region—wore little or no clothing. That lifestyle ended when the Indians were gathered around the Spanish missions, given new names and clothing, and put to work. The indigenous people had no resistance to the Europeans' diseases and did not adapt well to their way of life. Within 150 years, Florida's original Indians were wiped out.

As Europeans settled the other regions of what became the United States, similar struggles took place with other indigenous peoples. Florida was Spanish territory until 1821, and its harsh interior was practically empty of settlements. For at least a century, Indians who would not be ruled by whites slipped into Florida to live. At the same time, slaves who ran away from Southern plantations found safety among these people. Gradually, the groups banded together and came to be called

Seminoles. It is believed the word comes from the term *ishti semoli*, or "wild men," a phrase applied by the Creeks to these untamed people, many of whom were members of the Creek Confederation. At their peak, there were perhaps as many as 6,000 Seminoles in Florida. In three Seminole Wars—more a series of raids and skirmishes, really—the United States pressed its determination to settle Florida and wore down, killed, or resettled much of the Seminole population.

In the midst of these conflicts, a young Seminole leader emerged in Central Florida who became a legend of native American resistance. Born in Alabama, he was the son of a Creek Indian mother, and his given name was Billy Powell. Early in the 19th century, he came to Florida, where he took the name *Os-cin-ye-hula* (now Osceola) and led one of the last bands of Seminole raiders. He was captured in 1837, an event witnessed by Capt. Nathan S. Jarvis, a U.S. Army doctor, who

Seminole Indians from the Everglades, A Bride and Groom.

He's smoking a cigar, but she doesn't look too happy. This very fine vintage card is from the collection of Russell V. Hughes

left us a written account. The Army had arranged to meet with Osceola and some of his men—the Americans flying the white flag of truce. It was a trap.

> *Wishing to see him and hear the talk, I accompanied the Gen'l and his staff ... the Indians immediately gathered round us shaking hands with all the officers ... They [the Indians] thought they would come in and make peace with liberty to walk about. He [Osceola] was soon pointed out to me but I could have designated him by his looks as the principal man among them. His features indicated mildness and benevolence. A continuous smile play'd over his face, particularly when shaking hands with the officers present ... the Gen'l lifted a signal agreed upon and the troops closed in.*[1]

Osceola looked ill, the Army doctor thought, as they walked away toward St. Augustine, where the Indians were jailed in the fortress. In fact, Osceola died of malaria in a South Carolina prison within just one year. By 1858, there were only a few hundred Seminoles remaining in Florida. These slipped away into the sawgrass and the Everglades, where they were finally left in peace.

The Miccosukee
CREEK COUSINS

There were really two tribes of Seminole Indians: the Muskogee speakers and the Miccosukee speakers. Individuals in both tribes are the descendants of Creek Indians who drifted into Florida in the 18th and 19th centuries. The two tribes fought side by side in Central Florida during the Seminole Wars. Most in both groups agreed to be moved to the West in 1858. But a few hundred did not: the Muskogee speakers settled around Lake Okeechobee, and the Miccosukee speakers moved into the Everglades.

In the early part of the 20th century, the government passed laws protecting Florida's plumed wading birds. The feathers of these birds were being used on women's hats, so they had become a lucrative trading product for the Indians. At the same time, Florida's real development began. Roads were built, swamps were drained, and some of the Indians' hunting areas were no longer open to them.

The Miccosukee and the Seminole, ever adaptable, began building exhibition villages in Florida tourist locations. Some believed these exhibition villages were demeaning to the Indians, and in 1917, 1926, and 1935 the federal government set aside reservation land in Florida for them. In 1957, the Seminole Tribe (of mostly Muskogee speakers) incorporated and began to use the land to make money. In 1962, the Miccosukee did the same. Both tribes are now federally recognized.

Orange Avenue, from the collection of Russell V. Hughes.

A Brief Look at Orlando History

THE SMALL TOWN
WITH THE MEMORABLE NAME

I f it hadn't been for the Seminoles there may never have been an Orlando. During the Second Seminole War (1835-1842) General Thomas S. Jesup established a series of small forts a day's march apart—from Fort Monroe, near the site of the present-day Sanford, to Fort Brooke, near the site of the present-day Tampa. One of the forts in between was Fort Gatlin, just a few miles south of what is now downtown Orlando. It was just a small stockade, named after army surgeon Dr. John S. Gatlin, who was killed in one of the battles with the Indians. For several years, until the skirmishes with the Seminoles finally ended, settlers in Central Florida felt much more comfortable cultivating land near a stockade of U.S. soldiers. For a while, the entire settlement went by the name Fort Gatlin.

Aaron Jernigan was one of the first pioneers to settle near the fort in 1843. When he arrived, Florida was still a U.S. Territory, and the county he chose for homesteading carried the descriptive name Mosquito County. In 1845, Florida became a state and the name of the county was changed to Orange. Jernigan was elected to the new state legislature. When it appeared there might be further Seminole raids, he returned from the capital and built his own stockade. Eighty local residents retreated to its safety during the entire year of 1849. "As for life in the fort during that time," his daughter Martha wrote before her death in 1926, "there was only one fight. It was between two old women, and one had a butcher knife, and the other a firestick, but they did not get nearer than 20 or 30 feet of one another."[2] In 1850, when the settlement was granted its first post office, it was called "Jernigan."

A few years later, Orange County was carved up into several counties, and a vote was held to determine the new Orange County seat. One wily settler at Jernigan, James Gamble Speer, was determined that his town should prevail. Speer knew that all men over 21 who were in the militia were allowed to vote, and although there were no longer any soldiers at Fort Gatlin, there were some in nearby Sumter County. Mr. Speer hightailed it to Sumter, told the boys he needed their votes, and promised them a fine meal in return. Young men being as partial as they are to food, the soldiers trotted over the county line to vote and dine, and Mr. Speer's little village won the election.

Soon afterward, the new Orange County seat began going by the name "Orlando," and no one alive today is quite sure why. Eve Bacon, in her

As this vintage postcard shows, at the turn of the 20th century, even an Orlando street called "Main" (later renamed Magnolia) didn't rate a paving. Postcard courtesy of the Florida State Archives.

[2] *Orlando, A Centennial History*, Volume I, Eve Bacon

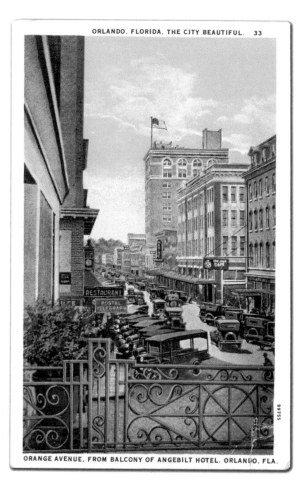

ORANGE AVENUE, FROM BALCONY OF ANGEBILT HOTEL, ORLANDO, FLA.

Orlando, A Centennial History (1975), quotes an undated paper in the Orlando Public Library archives handwritten by Claire Robinson, the daughter of one of James Gamble Speer's close friends:

> *The question of how it became to be named Orlando has been settled by Mr. B. M. Sims of Ocoee, Florida, in that Judge Speer told him that he named it for a man who once worked for him and whom he loved very much named Orlando, and Arthur Speer, his son ... told me the same thing.*

This contemporary account from Claire Robinson (Robinson Street is named after her father) is pretty convincing evidence. But since Judge Speer did not leave his own version behind, a number of others continue to circulate.

Multiple Choice

HOW ORLANDO GOT ITS NAME

A TOWN BY ANY OTHER NAME Judge Speer was said to have been fond of Shakespeare and to have named the town after the character Orlando in *As You Like It*.

HE LIES HENCE A Mr. Orlando was on his way to Tampa with his oxen, so the story goes, when unfortunately he died. Since he was buried near Fort Gatlin, people began saying: "There lies Orlando."

DO YOU BELIEVE BULL? Mr. F. K. Bull told Orlando newspapers in 1955 that he understood the city was named for his great-grandfather, Orlando Rees, an early Mosquito County settler.

OR DO YOU BELIEVE HULL? Eve Bacon does not cite her source for this in her 1975 book, but she reports that early settler William B. Hull said that he was at the meeting when the name was selected and that it was called Orlando because of its proximity to the grave of Orlando Reeves. Reeves was reportedly a U.S. solder, killed by the Seminole in 1835. According to Hull, Judge Speer said: "This place is often spoken of as 'Orlando's Grave.' Let's drop the word 'grave' and let the county seat be called Orlando." This is the version that has become most widely accepted. But as both Eve Bacon and authors Jim Robinson and Mark Andrews (*Flashbacks: The Story of Central Florida's Past*) note, the U.S. government has no record of a soldier named Orlando Reeves. Still, in 1939 students from Cherokee Junior High School placed a commemorative plaque at the southeast corner of Lake Eola, honoring this ephemeral lad: "In Whose Honor Our City of Orlando Was Named." The truth remains elusive. But once a story from history makes its way to a historical plaque, you might as well concede that it *could* have happened that way, and just leave it at that.

What kind of city was Orlando during its early years? For one thing, the shores of Lake Eola were so swampy that mules frequently bogged down in the muck up to their necks. Things were pretty wild. Thomas Homer Fuller, who came to Orlando after the Civil War, wrote home that he was surprised to find no church building in the city, which meant services had to be held out-of-doors. "A preacher came once a month to conduct services," he wrote. "The boys took their dogs to Sunday School, and they often got to fighting and broke up the meeting."[3]

By 1880, Orlando still wasn't much to look at, as Mr. Mahlon Gore told a group of old-timers in 1908:

> I walked over from Sanford, taking two days to make the trip. The sand was deep and the last end of the road stretched out unaccountably long. At about the present intersection of Magnolia Avenue and Livingston Street, was a little house owned and occupied by a clergyman named Beveridge, pastor of the Presbyterian church. And a block to the east, discernible through the trees, was another, the home of E. W. Spier. No other buildings were in sight, but meeting a man on horseback, I inquired how far it was to Orlando; the man … looked me over for several seconds, sized me up for a tenderfoot, and then

Orange Ave., Looking South, Orlando, Fla.

Another view of Orange Avenue, courtesy of the Orange County Regional History Center.

[3] *Orlando, A Centennial History*, Volume I, Eve Bacon

replied, "Why you d--- fool, you're in Orlando now." There were just two houses in sight. I had come fourteen hundred miles to get to Orlando; I wanted to go home right then.[4]

Carl Dann, who was born in Orlando in 1885 and later developed Dubsdread County Club, wrote that he recalled the Orlando of his youth as having "very few houses and stores, but plenty of saloons." Another pioneer remembered when Orlando's Lake Dot was called "that mud hole with the big alligator."

The narrow-gauge Orlando & Winter Park Railway[5] began running in 1889, and was immediately nicknamed The Dinky Line. Residents called its two wood-burning steam engines "The Coffee Pot" and "The Tea Pot." The one-way trip between Orlando and Winter Park was five miles and cost 25 cents. The Dinky was so notoriously slow that one student at Rollins College in Winter Park claimed he got off one day in frustration, walked to Lake Ivanhoe—on the edge of downtown Orlando—did some homework, dozed off, was awakened by the train, and hopped on it for the last mile to the Orlando station. Rollins students were the bane of the railroad's engineers' existence. For fun, they would soap the tracks, and the

This is an original pass for the Dinky Line, dated 1889, from the Department of College Archives and Special Collections, Olin Library, Rollins College.

little engine would spin its wheels until everyone got out and shoveled sand onto the tracks. When The Dinky was purchased in 1892 by the Florida Central and Peninsular Railroad—the F.C.&P.—the line was just naturally called "Friends Come & Push."[6]

In 1883, Orlando installed its first sidewalks. In 1908, there were two landmarks: Orlando Water and Light put up the first electric poles; and the city ruled that police officers could, during the hottest months of the summer, appear on duty without their coats. It was the first recorded official concession to the kind of comfortable lifestyle that would one day make Central Florida famous.

---

[4] *History of Orange County Florida*, William F. Blackman.

[5] In various sources over the years, the railway has been identified with an "and" in its title, with a "—," and with the ampersand used here. It has been called a railway and a railroad. The version I'm using here is the one written on the ticket (above) found in the archives of Rollins College.

[6] "The Dinky", by Judge Donald A. Cheney, Rollins Alumni *Record*, October 1967.

John Otto Fries in a photograph from the Orange County Regional History Center.

John Otto Fries
ORLANDO'S FIRST SURVEYOR

John Otto Fries (1838-1931) arrived in Sanford (then called Mellonville) on Christmas Eve 1871. He was from Uppsala, Sweden, and had a wife and two young daughters. Yet, at the age of 33, he had caught the pioneer bug and come alone to this rough new land to homestead. He planned to send for his family when he got settled. We don't know how he spent that first Christmas in Mellonville, but on the day after Christmas, he hired a fellow named George Lewis to take him by wagon the 25 miles to Orlando for ten dollars. The wagon was pulled by four mules, and its progress was slow. When they got to the present-day Longwood—about ten miles from Orlando—the harness broke, and the driver got down and scratched his head trying to figure out what to do. Otto Fries dug into his satchel for a pair of suspenders and some leather shoelaces, fixed the harness, and got the wagon back on its way.

Fries looked around Orlando for a couple of days and on December 29, he decided to go back to Mellonville. George Lewis asked him if he'd like a ride for the price of nine dollars—offering Fries the one-dollar discount for the work he'd done repairing the harness. Fries said no, he figured he'd just walk, thanks very much. The wagon left without him and Fries started out on foot. After a few hours he passed Lewis, and arrived in Mellonville about three hours ahead of him. This Swede seemed made to survive in Florida.

He was a well-educated man. One of the men he met during those first few months told him that the area could use a good surveyor. Fries had studied engineering in Stockholm and thought this sounded like a pretty good job for him. So he set about homesteading some land near Oviedo and began hiring himself out to survey the plats of the new homesteads springing up around him in Orange County. He saved his earnings to bring his family to Florida. In the spring of 1873, he wrote his daughter, 6-year-old Christina, whom he always called Kena:

Now I will tell you how many animals I have ... First, I have now a large rooster and 14 hens and then I have 11 small chickens ... [They] are so lively and happy and run along with their mother and hunt worms and seed on the ground. And when I come out to them and call: biddy, biddy, all come running as fast as their little feet can run and pick the grain I bring them. Just think when you come here, then you will have to feed them, they are not at all afraid, they eat out of my hands if one does not scare them.[7]

This is a page from one of John Otto Fries' surveying notebooks.

For his little girl, he was painting a picture of the life that would be ahead of her in the new land. Not long afterward, in 1873, his family joined him. Ten years later they all moved into Orlando, when Fries was elected Orange County Surveyor.

[7] Unpublished letter in the archives of the Orange County Regional History Center.

His directive was to draw up the first map of the county. On February 3, 1888, he posted this notice:

> Having for ten years made necessary preparations I am now making a map of Orange county [sic], Florida. The size will be 6 feet by 5 feet, not including the border. It will show all townships, sections, and quarter section lines, with their jogs and irregularities, all towns, churches, school houses, post offices, lakes, rivers, streams, ponds, swamps, roads, etc., in fact a full topography of the county. To show all the improvements and names of the residents in general would take too much time, and would also crowd the map too much. But knowing that there are many persons wishing to have their places and full names on this map I have finally decided to give any body an opportunity to have his wish complied with. Any body sending me, before April 1st, their name, with one dollar enclosed in the letter, will have their improvements and names on this map. I will visit every place to myself locate the improvements and residences. Very respectfully,
>
> J. O. Fries, County Surveyor[8]

Imagine the job of surveying Orange County in 1888! Fries, who by then was 50 years old, had to walk every mile of the county to create the map he did. But he was not one to let obstacles discourage him, and within two years the map was completed. In 1900, when he was 62 years old, he was sent to South Florida to take the first census of the Seminole Indians, and he tramped down there into swamps and hammocks most Floridians had never seen. One of his assistants said that when Fries was well into his 80s, he continued to survey, and when he came to a river or stream, he simply stripped down, tied his clothing into a bundle, put it on his head, swam across, and got dressed again on the other side. On into the 20th century, his survey marks and land corners continued to be in use. He died in Orlando in 1931 at the age of 93, having worked until seven years before his death.

His daughter Kena had some kind of physical disability. Contemporary accounts describe her as "crippled" but never make clear what the disability was. Her younger sister, Eva, married; but, Kena did not, and lived on alone in the family's house at 1023 East Livingston after the deaths of her mother and father. In 1938, at the age of 71, she wrote a little book of local history called *Orlando in the Long, Long, Ago … And Now*[9]. "It brought me money enough to re-roof my house," she

---

[8] Copy of original notice in the archives of the Orange County Regional History Center.
[9] Tyn Cobb Florida Press, Orlando, 1938

said. The book became the inspiration for Orlando's "Centennial and Pioneer Days" celebration in April 1942. She appeared at all the events, and when they were over, she retreated to the old house, her garden, and her collection of cats.

John Otto Fries and his daughter Kena in the backyard of their Orlando home shortly before his death in 1931. From the Orange County Regional History Center.

The garden was overflowing with rare plants collected by her father during his walks across the state. She died in 1945 at the age of 77—a woman who had lived from the days of homesteads and mule transport through to the atomic age. When she died, the *Orlando Morning Sentinel* wrote: "Funeral Arrangements have not been completed, but they will give Orlando opportunity to pay fitting tribute to Kena Fries, a fine woman and one who always thought of others before herself." Before she died, she made arrangements for all her father's surveying notebooks and other papers to go to Orange County, so researchers in future centuries could learn about the Orlando she and her father had known in the long, long ago.

School kids. A vintage postcard from the Florida State Archives.

The Town That Freedom Built
EATONVILLE

t the end of the Civil War, a number of former slaves from other parts of the South moved to Florida to begin their lives anew. In the Orlando area, a relatively large group of African Americans settled near the shores of Lake Sybelia (which at that time went by the unglamorous name St. John's Hole) in Maitland. Three Union officers were among the leaders of the City of Maitland, and they encouraged African Americans to take part in civic affairs.

In 1880, the African American citizens began a movement to form their own town. Joseph E. Clark, who was African American, appealed to philanthropist Lewis Lawrence, who purchased 22 acres from Maitland's Captain Josiah Eaton in 1881.

During the days of segregation clubs like this one catered to Orlando's African American population. Photo courtesy of the Department of College Archives and Special Collections, Olin Library, Rollins College.

The Hungerford School was prestigious, and it has always been in Eatonville. It is unclear why this school bulletin for 1940-1941 identifies its location as "Maitland." This bulletin is from the Department of College Archives and Special Collections, Olin Library, Rollins College. They have a number of these bulletins in their archives.

THE ROBERT
HUNGERFORD
VOCATIONAL SCHOOL
MAITLAND, FLORIDA

The Headmaster and Mrs. John E. Hall

BULLETIN FOR 1940-41

Lawrence, who was white, gave 10 acres to the African Methodist Episcopal Church and 12 acres to Joe Clark. These first acres, about 10 miles north of Orlando, became the foundation of Eatonville, incorporated in 1887, the nation's first town founded by and for African Americans. In 1889, R. C. Calhoun founded the Robert Hungerford Normal & Industrial School in Eatonville, which for many years was the only first-rate private academy for African Americans in Florida. Eatonville gradually expanded to include 112 acres.

Eatonville's third mayor was the Rev. John Hurston, who moved to Eatonville from Nostasulga, Alabama, with his wife and six children. The baby of the family (until three more children were born in Eatonville) was daughter Zora Neale Hurston, born in 1891. Zora Neale Hurston attended Hungerford, went on to Howard University in Washington, DC, and also studied at Barnard College, in New York City. In New York she met the poet Langston Hughes, and became a part of what is now called the Harlem Renaissance. She had become a writer and set her autobiography, *Dust Tracks on a Road*, in Eatonville. Most of her books, including *Their Eyes Were Watching God*, *Dust Tracks on a Road*, and *Jonah's Gourd Vine*, continue to be in print today.

In 1989, the City of Eatonville was awarded a grant from the State of Florida to explore its history. The annual Zora Neale Hurston Festival of the Arts and Humanities, established that year, has become a premier three-day national cultural event. Also that year, Eatonville was placed on the National Register of Historic Places. Though none of its original buildings remain, "The Town That Freedom Built" continues to be of national importance.

This is a very rare postcard of students in a class at Hungerford. They're learning the printing trade. The vintage card is from the collection of Russell V. Hughes.

Eatonville has now established Eatonville's Heritage Trail, a walking tour through the town's history. Maps are available though the concierge desks at most hotels in Central Florida, or you can contact Eatonville Town Hall, 332 East Kennedy Boulevard, Eatonville, Florida 32751, **407-623-1313**. For more information on the annual Zora Neale Hurston Festival (which usually takes place in January), contact Preserve Eatonville Community, Inc., 227 East Kennedy Boulevard, Eatonville, Florida 32750, **407-647-3307**, or log on to www.zoranealehurstonfestival.com. The Zora Neale Hurston National Museum of Fine Arts is another interesting stop in Eatonville. It is open Monday through Friday, 9:00 a.m. to 4:00 p.m., 227 E. Kennedy Boulevard, Eatonville, Florida 32751, **407-647-3307**.

Orlando's Pineries
PITCHING IN

Florida once led the nation in the production of tar, resin, and turpentine, all of which come from the pitch of the pine tree. The business was worth about $200,000 in the State of Florida in 1890, and had grown to $7.8 million by 1900. Between 1905 and 1923, the pineries and turpentine stills employed more than 6,000 men in Florida each year, and Orlando—rich in native pines—was one of the centers of the business. The labor wasn't always voluntary. For many years, the industry employed convict labor. The companies also paid off the fines of vagrants and then charged them for transportation to the pineries as well as for room and board and other living expenses. Many of the men found not only that they were *not* making a profit, but also that they would never be able to work off their debts. They worked from "can't to can't," according to one veteran, that is, they worked from "can't see anything in the morning 'til can't see anything at night." The sap from pine trees was harvested beginning in March of each year. After six years, a pine tree was "sapped" and no longer productive. Gradually, most of Orlando's trees were tapped, sapped, and cut down. In 1919, the state outlawed convict labor at the camps, and by the 1930s, the center of tar and turpentine production had moved back up to Georgia. Today, 90% of the world's turpentine products come from Portugal, and the remaining Orlando pine trees produce nothing but shade.

This is an Orlando pinery near an orange grove. The turpentine stills were put at the edges of lakes because water was used in the process. In the picture, Orlando's Lake Concord is at left and Lake Ivanhoe is at right.

PICKING ORANGES IN FLORIDA

Florida Citrus
SUNSHINE ON A TREE

C itrus put Central Florida on the map long before tourism did. The roots of the orange, so to speak, are Asian. The name of the fruit comes from the Sanskrit word *nagarunga* which means "fruit loved by elephants." The word then evolved into the Arabic word *narandj*, which English speakers corrupted into orange. The Spanish brought the first oranges to Florida in the early 16th century—and that should be no surprise since two of the most popular orange varieties today are called by the Spanish names *Valencia* and *Seville*.

By 1565, orange trees were flourishing near St. Augustine, and native Americans spread them further as they walked their traditional paths, discarding seeds from the fruit they were eating. When the English arrived in the 19th century, they thought these old orange trees were native and began grafting sweeter varieties to their trunks. By 1826, a million oranges were being shipped each year from St. Augustine to England, and when Orlando residents voted to name their county Orange in 1845, the name reflect- ed the area's growing specialty. When the railroads arrived in Florida in the late 19th century, the citrus business really took off. For the first time, growers could move their fruit all over the United States in a matter of days. Orlando, which had 200 residents in 1880, had 6,000 residents five years later, and citrus was the reason.

Central Florida is not above the freeze line, as early settlers believed. Hard freezes in the 19th century damaged trees and destroyed crops. Some growers sold out, and many moved farther south. One Orange County grower, who had paid $40,000 for his grove, traded it for a ticket back home to England.

The invention of orange concentrate in the mid-20th century changed the citrus business again. Orange juice moved ahead of fresh fruit as the product of primary importance. Orlando became the state's largest center for orange juice processing.

In the last decades of the 20th century, with the growth of tourism, thousands of people moved to Orlando, and acres of groves were sold for housing. In spite of that and in spite of the occasional freeze, the counties surrounding the Central Florida tourism corridor still produce nearly one quarter of Florida's annual citrus crop, which totals between 200 and 300 million boxes of fruit. Orange County itself isn't quite as orange as it used to be, producing only about 1 percent of the total. But Polk County—just south of Walt Disney World—leads the state, joined by Lake, Osceola, Brevard, Volusia, and Seminole counties in adding significantly to Florida's annual harvest.

There are those who will tell you the taste of citrus grown in Florida is the best in the world. That's one of the reasons citrus remains a multibillion dollar business in Florida nearly half a millennium after the first orange tree came ashore in the hands of a Spanish explorer.

> If you want to tour a citrus grove during your visit to the Orlando area, contact the Florida Department of Citrus, P.O. Box 148, Lakeland, Florida 33802-0148, **863-499-2500**. Or log on to www.floridajuice.com. There are lots of choices for tours in the Central Florida region.

FLAMINGO ORANGE GROVES

PICKING ORANGES FOR YOU AND YOUR FRIENDS

The San Juan Hotel could be found at 32 North Orange Avenue, and the Angebilt (right) was just across the street at 37 North Orange Avenue. The two hotels carried on a constant rivalry. Aren't these great-looking postcards with the little cars running around in front of each hotel on an otherwise empty Orange Avenue? Courtesy of the Florida State Archives.

HOTELS OF BYGONE DAYS

THE RIVALS   The **San Juan Hotel** was built in downtown Orlando, at 32 North Orange Avenue, in the 1880s, the height of the growth of the citrus business. It was originally three stories tall, which made it the largest building in Orlando at that time. In the 1890s, chewing gum king Harry Beeman bought the hotel and added two stories to accommodate Orlando's continued growth. Streetcars pulled by mules transported guests from the Orlando train station along Orange Avenue to the hotel. The San Juan wasn't far from the city jail, and guests were known to go upstairs and watch out the windows when they heard there would be a hanging. During its heyday, the hotel housed the offices of the Florida Symphony and played host to Babe Ruth, Leo Durocher, and Hank Greenberg. It became the only Orlando hotel to survive in one location for an entire century. But the distinction didn't last: the San Juan was torn down in 1980.

The **Angebilt Hotel** ("bilt" by J. F. Ange) went up in 1923, right across the street from the San Juan, at 37 North Orange Avenue on the site of the old Rosalind

Club. With 11 floors, the Angebilt could lay claim to being Orlando's first "sky-scraper." (Almost immediately, the owners of the San Juan Hotel added an eight-story tower, so it too could scrape the sky.) The Junior League met at the Angebilt, and Orlando High held its dances on the sky roof. One day, just after the Angebilt opened its doors, a chauffeured limousine arrived carrying three men. The chauffeur registered the men, who remained in the car out of sight. Young assistant manager Tyndale Cobb, Jr., was suspicious. It wasn't until the next day, as the men were departing, that someone said, "Hey, that's Henry Ford!" It seems that Henry Ford (1863-1947), Harvey Firestone (1868-1938), and Thomas Edison (1847-1931) had stopped at the Angebilt on their way to Edison's home in Fort Myers. Only the walls of the Angebilt know what those three giants talked about that night.

A few years later, a fellow called Henry "Dare Devil" Roland—a sort of Spiderman of his day—climbed the 11-story exterior of the Angebilt. The newly licensed radio station, WDBO, broadcast its first "live remote" from the event. The hotel was renovated in the 1980s and turned into 85,000 square feet of office space. Today it has a fast-food restaurant on the ground floor, but its distinctive iron entrance canopy remains a sign of its historic past.

THE SAN JUAN HOTEL, ORLANDO, FLA.

This vintage postcard shows the San Juan Hotel
before the eight-story tower was added.
Postcard courtesy of the Florida State Archives.

Summerlin Hotel This was Orlando's first rooming house, built by city father Jacob Summerlin. He had helped Orlando become the county seat; but, because there was no hotel, visiting judges, cattle buyers, and everybody else who visited stayed at Summerlin's house. He got tired of all the company and, in 1873, built the four-room hotel (later expanded) at 120 East Washington Street. In 1881, the manager sent a request to the City: "… to keep on the ground of the Summerlin House a pig pen for the consumption of swill & etc." The Summerlin survived the pig, but not the ravages of time. It was razed after World War II.

The Tremont Hotel This was another of Orlando's earliest hotels, built in 1892 at the corner of Magnolia Avenue (then Main Street) and Church Street. It was built on the site of one of Orlando's earliest cemeteries—something not widely publicized for obvious reasons. The hotel also incorporated parts of a building that had once been a school and a church—hence the origin of the name Church Street. The old hotel came down in 1956.

The Tremont Hotel, Orlando, Fla.

The Orange Court Hotel (later the Orange Court Motor Hotel) This one lasted until 1988. Consequently, many locals still remember it. It was built in 1920 at 650 North Orange Avenue, and ads said it was "as gracious as the Waldorf Astoria." By the 1960s it was mostly an apartment hotel for seniors. When it was torn down in 1988, the late Hugh McKean, founder of the Charles Hosmer Morse Museum in Winter Park, salvaged its neon sign, which remains in the museum's collection.

O.62.   ORLANDO. FLORIDA. THE CITY BEAUTIFUL.

ORANGE COURT HOTEL.

The Orange Court in her prime was a sight to behold. She had an indoor pool and everything! The postcard above is from the Rollins archives. The card below is from the archives of the Orange County Regional History Center.

COLONIAL SWIMMING POOL — COLONIAL ORANGE COURT HOTEL — ORLANDO, FLORIDA

*From left to right, Walt Disney, General William E. "Joe" Potter,
and Roy O. Disney at the 1965 Orlando press conference
announcing "Project Florida."*

"Project Florida"
HOW THE THEME PARKS CAME

arly in 1965, someone started buying up big stretches of property south of Orlando. It didn't happen all at once, and none of the names of the buyers sounded familiar. But it was evident that someone was quietly putting together something really big. Reporters at the *Orlando Sentinel* got wind of it, and they began writing about the mystery. Was it going to be a high-tech company? Would it be a big military base? Nobody was talking. Then, a *Sentinel* editor and reporter named Emily Bavar (later Emily Bavar Kelly) got an invitation that paid off.

"I went on a junket," she said many years later. "It was a trip in celebration of Disneyland's tenth anniversary, and we were ushered into Mr. Disney's office and told we could ask questions. When it was my turn, I asked Mr. Disney if he was the one who was buying up these 20,000 acres, and it stunned him so, it made me think maybe he was."[10] Emily Bavar Kelly told me in a telephone conversation 31 years later, that she had asked the question purely on a hunch.[11]

---

[10] Interview in the archives of the Walt Disney World Resort, used in a 25th anniversary video I produced for the company in 1996.

[11] I interviewed Emily Bavar Kelly in 1996. She died July 2003, and the headline on her *Orlando Sentinel* obituary read: "Journalist who broke Disney story dies at 88."

"He said he wasn't doing it. But then he went on, and it turned out he knew how many tourists came here, how much it rained all summer; he knew entirely too much about the area not to have a reason. Yes, he denied it. No, I didn't believe him." Bavar's stories were headlined "Disney Hedges Big Question" and "Girl Reporter Convinced by Walt Disney." Emily Bavar had guessed the truth.

Walter Elias Disney, born December 5, 1901, had established a very successful animation studio in Hollywood, beginning in 1923. The company's success was built on the shoulders of his best-known character, Mickey Mouse. In the 1950s, Walt Disney was quick to seize on the enormous marketing power of television. He produced a network television program for children, "The Mickey Mouse Club" (ABC-TV 1955-1959), and used his Sunday night network television program, "Disneyland" (ABC-TV 1954-1958) to introduce his animated films to a new

November 11,1965 "Project Florida" was announced. This was probably the last time the Disney Company gave a press conference in a movie theater "Off Property."

generation. He also used the show to promote his first theme park (while he was building it), which was not coincidentally named Disneyland. When the Disneyland theme park opened in 1955 in Anaheim, California, it featured rides and attractions based on Disney's animation, his movies, and his television programs. We don't know if Walt Disney ever used the work "synergy," but he sure knew what it meant.

Ten years after the opening of Disneyland, it appeared Walt Disney had big plans in mind for Florida. With the property transfers just about wrapped up and the speculation coming very close to the truth, Walt Disney made it official. On November 11, 1965, in Orlando, with his brother Roy at his side, in the somewhat humble surroundings of the Wometco Park Theater, Disney announced plans for his "Project Florida." "After ten years of Disneyland, with 20-20 hindsight, you begin to wonder what you would do if you were starting from scratch," he told the audience, and then he smiled. "And after viewing the property today, believe me, we are starting from scratch."[12]

[12] Video of the press conference in the archives of the Walt Disney World Resort.

In all, the Walt Disney Company bought 27,000 acres in Florida, or about 43 square miles of land. Walt Disney later announced on his television program that he was planning to build something completely different this time—something he planned to call the Experimental Prototype Community of Tomorrow, or EPCOT, where people would live, work, and play in a city of the future. He certainly had enough land for it.

Walt Disney at left and Florida governor Haydon Burns, center, at the 1965 Disney press conference and reception. Note the woman with her back to the camera wearing a mink stole, always a rare sight in Florida! Haydon Burns was governor just from 1965 to 1967 due to a new Florida law that changed the cycle of gubernatorial elections.

But he didn't have enough time. Just a year later, in December 1966, Walt Disney died at the age of 65. It was left to the Board of Directors of the Walt Disney Company and to Roy O. Disney to decide what to do.

What they decided to do was move forward. They named the project Walt Disney World in honor of the man whose dream it had been. In 1967, they broke ground for what was then the largest commercial construction project in the world. Under the direction of General William E. "Joe" Potter, who had once been the administrator of the Panama Canal Zone, construction workers drained swampy land and created a series of lakes and canals to channel the water. They graded the property, built broad roadways, and created a large buffer zone around the property to keep the outside world—and the competition—at a distance.

From left, Don Tatum, Roy O. Disney, Jack Sayers, and General W. E. "Joe" Potter take a look at the Disney property south of Orlando.

The work, on property twice the size of the island of Manhattan, was done with such foresight that it made possible 30 years of development on the site without the need for any major re-engineering. Another former military man, Admiral Joe Fowler (1894-1993), handled the construction of the resort's first theme park and its hotels. The work completed by Fowler and Potter was so extraordinary that Disney now honors them with engineering scholarships in their names at the University of Central Florida.

October 1, 1971, was opening day for the Magic Kingdom at Walt Disney World and for the Contemporary and the Polynesian resorts. One man, now an executive with Walt Disney World, told me he was sent down to the shoulder of I-4 that day to count the cars going by. "And since there weren't that many, it wasn't a very hard job!" That may have been the last slow day for traffic on I-4. In the coming years, Disney and the theme park business would

The Walt Disney World project was the biggest construction project of its kind in 1967, on property twice the size of the island of Manhattan.

bring millions of visitors to Orlando and grow to dominate the Central Florida economy. After October 1, 1971, Orlando, the once-quiet little citrus town, was on its way to becoming one of the most visited tourist destinations in the world.

The Magic Kingdom at Walt Disney World on opening day October 1, 1971. The shrubbery has grown up a bit since then.

All of the photos in this section are from the Florida State Archives, Commerce Collection.

©2003 Universal Orlando

©2003 SeaWorld of Florida

©2003 SeaWorld of Florida

©Disney 2003

VISITING THE THEME PARKS

©Disney 2003

VISITING THE THEME PARKS

The Big One

THE WALT DISNEY WORLD RESORT®

There are now four theme parks at the Walt Disney World Resort:

The Magic Kingdom Opened in 1971, it is the most popular park at WDW. Set on 107 acres, it could hold the original Disneyland in Anaheim, California, inside its parking lot. Its icon is Cinderella Castle.

©Disney 2003

©Disney 2003

Epcot An acronym invented by Walt Disney: the letters stand for Experimental Prototype Community of Tomorrow. Once called "EPCOT Center," the capital letters and the word "Center" have been deleted from the name. Opened in 1982, the park is set on 300 acres. Its icon is the silver sphere called Spaceship Earth.

Disney-MGM Studios Opened in 1989, it is second to the Magic Kingdom in the number of visitors it attracts. The park's icon was the Chinese Theater, but beginning in 2001, Mickey's Sorcerer's Hat became the park's new symbol.

©Disney 2003

©Disney 2003

Disney's Animal Kingdom At 500 acres, this park, opened in 1998, is technically the largest one at WDW, though most of that acreage is set aside for the park's permanent residents—the animals. The icon here is the Tree of Life, a man-made tree that features intricately carved creatures on its base.

WDW LINGO

Cast Member   WDW Employee. Each wears a name tag which also identifies his or her hometown.

Guest   A person visiting WDW.

On Stage   Cast Members are On Stage wherever and whenever they greet Guests.

On Property   Anything within the borders of WDW.

Throughput   This is another name for capacity. It means the number of people who can be put through a ride or show each hour.

BGM   Background music. It's ubiquitous at WDW.

Underutilized   Not crowded.

Priority Seating   Reservations.

Quick Service   Fast food.

Audio-Animatronic   A word invented by Walt Disney, it describes stand-alone puppetlike figures that move and talk.

Guest Satisfaction   What the Walt Disney World Resort strives for every single day. The company takes frequent surveys on this subject, called Guest Satisfaction Measurements (GSMs).

Horticulture   This is the WDW name for the department that does the gardening and the landscaping at the Walt Disney World Resort. Horticulture contributes greatly to WDW's high GSM ratings.

©Disney 2003

The author (left) and her sister on their first visit to a Disney theme park, long ago in a land far away. Where are the other Guests do you suppose? Dig those crazy white socks.

THE ABSOLUTELY ESSENTIAL MAGIC KINGDOM

FASTPASS In the late 1990s, WDW began getting signals that the wait times for attractions were making Guests unhappy. The company came up with its FASTPASS® solution, and it is now working well. Go to the attraction you're interested in visiting, insert your valid ticket into the FASTPASS machine, and receive a FASTPASS, which gives you a 1-hour window during which you will be able to enter the attraction with little or no wait time. On the rarest and absolute busiest of days it is possible for FASTPASS to max out, so go early to your favorite rides. One hitch: you cannot do a circuit of the park and get a FASTPASS for each of your favorite attractions and then decide later which ones to use. You must use your FASTPASS or wait for it to expire, before you can get another one. Each FASTPASS now has the time written on it at which you can get another. When you get a FASTPASS, you are making a reservation. FASTPASS helps to "load manage" these rides by not issuing you a second reservation until you've used your first one—or until that reservation has expired.

Stamp of Approval You can leave the Magic Kingdom (in fact any of the parks) and return the same day, but to do so you must have your hand stamped upon exit.

Shop 'Til You Drop There are at least 43 different places to shop within the MK. The post-shows at many attractions spill out into shopping areas, so, it is fairly unlikely you will be able to resist the impulse to acquire more stuff. To lighten your load, you can have your packages delivered to Package Pickup near the front entrance. There will be lots of other people also picking up their packages at closing time. Think of it as you would valet parking, with 50,000 people all wanting their cars at the same time and schedule your package picking up plans perceptively.

Times Guide & New Information This is an information sheet printed daily that includes all the times for everything. These times change frequently, so be sure and pick up one along with your park map at the park entrance, or at any Guest Services station.

Character Connection The Times Guide & New Information sheet has a list of Character Greeting times within the park. Some of the restaurants specialize in what is called a "Character Breakfast" (a meal with Mickey, Minnie, and friends), and these are very popular with children. Ask at Guest Relations, or call **407-939-3463** for details on Character Dining.

Shows, Parades and Fireworks Magic Kingdom parades, entertainments, and fireworks shows are always changing, as are their times and frequency. Check your Times Guide & New Information sheet for the latest information.

©Disney 2003

E-Tickets Guests staying at Disney resorts should ask about **E-Ride Nights**, a program that allows some Guests (on certain nights) to remain in the park after hours. The term "E-Ride" has its origins in Disney theme park history. When the parks first opened, visitors bought packages of tickets that included A, B, C, D, and E tickets. These were redeemed at rides that had these letter designations. There were lots of A's, fewer B's, and so on, with each package including the least number of E's, which were always for the best rides. Today, when people say, "That's a real E-ticket," this is what they mean. Unless, of course, they work for the airlines.

Don't Belly Up, Boys In deference to Disney tradition, no alcohol is served within the Magic Kingdom. The other parks do serve alcohol.

WDW Horticulture

YOU CAN LEARN A LOT OF THINGS FROM THE FLOWERS

There is so much going on around you at WDW, you might not take the time to stop and smell the roses. You really should, as there are 13,000 rose bushes On Property for your visual and olfactory pleasure. There are also more than 2 million shrubs, 2-3 million annuals, and 100,000 trees. As mentioned earlier, WDW calls its landscaping department "Horticulture," and this department employs more than 600 Cast Members to tend its 3,500 acres of gardens. Most of

these gardeners work in the wee, small hours of the morning, completing their work about the time you arrive at WDW. Topiary—the art of clipping shrubs and training vines into ornamental shapes—is an award-winning specialty of WDW Horticulture. There are more than 200 different topiary sculptures On Property for Guests to enjoy. Disney also employs some Integrated Pest Management techniques to avoid the overuse of pesticides. It is a tribute to the Horticulture team that every single flower bed at the Walt Disney World Resort is always absolutely perfect.

©Disney 2003

©Disney 2003

And Away We Go!
THE MAGIC KINGDOM

Planning Your Visit   The popularity of this park means that during special events and holidays the daily number of visitors can reach as high as 55,000. I don't know where you are from, but that is more people than live in my hometown. If you visit during the Christmas holidays, for example, or at the height of the summer vacation season in August, you'll be joining a large crowd. If you like crowds, you'll be just fine. If this bothers you, come during off-peak times for a much more enjoyable visit. If you can't do that, do a little planning to ease your stress. Be a contrarian: if everyone is watching the parade, use that time to visit your favorite attractions. If the wait times will be long in the restaurants at lunch or dinner, bring a snack and eat your major meal after you leave the park. If people are sleeping in, come to the park early. If people leave at dinnertime and come back later, come at dinnertime, and leave when they return. Buy a ticket that will give you enough flexibility that you won't feel under pressure to stay at the park beyond your ability to enjoy it, just because you feel you have to get your money's worth.

> Locals have the option of visiting during the slowest times of the year. Two of the best times are the weeks between Labor Day in early September and Thanksgiving in late November; and the weeks between New Year's Day and early March. The weather is great during both of these times, and the crowds are the smallest of the year. Cast Members are happy to see you, and you'll get even better than the usual excellent service.

Starting Out No matter when you choose to visit, the first thing that will make your day easier is to arrive early. Even if the park is not scheduled to open until 9:00 a.m., you will do yourself no harm by arriving at the parking lot at 8:00 a.m. It will still take you some time to get to the front gate from the lot, and if there is a good crowd, Disney will open the gates earlier than scheduled. That allows Guests to get a cup of coffee and a snack before the official "rope drop" that begins the day.

Coming and Going Hours of operation vary from day to day, and season to season. Disney has an extraordinarily accurate formula for predicting how many people will be in each park on any given day; there is an entire WDW department devoted to these projections. If there will be big crowds—the parks open earlier and stay open later. Smaller crowds—shorter hours. These formulas also

Even if you take the scenic route through Florida, it pays to leave early for your day at the theme parks. Vintage postcard courtesy of the Florida State Archives.

*The Ticket and Transportation Center of the Magic Kingdom on
October 1, 1971. It is a rare photo of the parking lot looking so empty!
Photo courtesy of the Florida State Archives.*

impact the number of Cast Members on duty, as well as the number and times of shows. Call **407-824-4321** for park hours or visit the Disney Web site at www.disneyworld.com.

En Route If you are driving, the signs on I-4 and all the nearby roadways (as far away as Orlando International Airport) will direct you to the proper exits to take for each Disney park. Exit 64 off I-4 is the correct exit for the Magic Kingdom, but the secret is: any Disney exit will do. The Disney roadway system is so good that if you just get onto Disney property (On Property) and watch the signs, you will find the appropriate turn-off for anyplace you want to go. If you miss one exit, you will find the roadway is like a big great circle route, and if you are patient, another exit to your destination will come around again soon. (I know this because, when I worked at Disney, I would sometimes daydream on my way to meetings— the property is huge, after all—and I would *occasionally* miss my turn-off. Now it can be told.) If you are staying On Property you will find free transportation to all the parks. Most hotels and motels in the region also provide shuttle service.

Greetings Follow the signs to the Magic Kingdom, and you will reach something that looks like a large tollgate. Here you will meet your first Cast Member, whom you will pay for a parking pass. Prices vary depending on whether you bring an RV, a limo, or the family van.

©Disney 2003

The Ticket and Transportation Center today.

Parking This is the world's best-organized parking lot. A Cast Member directs you to your spot. The cars are parked in such a way that you cannot be blocked by another vehicle, so you can return to the lot and depart whenever you choose. Make a note of the row in which you leave your car. There are spaces for 11,000 vehicles in this lot, and you will need a means of finding your way back. Lock your car: this is a theme park, not heaven. Leave nothing in your vehicle that can be damaged by heat: temperatures can be in the 90s°F (at least 32°C) in the summer in Florida, and the temperature inside a vehicle can easily rise to 150°F (65.5°C). This temperature can melt lipstick, make food inedible, and even cause plastic dashboards to bubble.

> **Trams** From your vehicle you will be directed to walk to the nearest tram stop just steps away. The trams are open-air, and come around one after the other, so don't worry if you miss one. The Cast Members who operate them will take you to the Transportation and Ticket Center (TTC). (Watch your head on the trams: they aren't designed to allow adults to stand up in them.)

The MK TTC If you need to buy tickets, this is where you will do that. If you already have tickets, you will present them here. If you are taking WDW transportation, it will bring you directly here. Once you have your ticket, walk through the gates and … you still have one more ride before you arrive at the Magic Kingdom. There is a really nice picnic spot at the TTC that Guests can use any time they wish.

Almost There You can now go to the right and take the monorail—which is generally the quickest route—or you can go to the left and take one of the ferryboats—which I think is the nicest way to go. (One of the ferries is named for Admiral Joe Fowler, the Navy man in charge of the Magic Kingdom's construction.) The Seven Seas Lagoon, which you cross on the ferry, is one of the many man-made bodies of water at the Walt Disney World Resort. From it you can see several Disney resort hotels, including the Polynesian and the Disney Yacht and Beach Club. Whether you take the monorail or the ferry, you are taking a ride that was intentionally designed to separate you from the hustle and bustle of the parking and ticket-selling operations and move you gradually into the pixie-dust-sprinkled world of the Magic Kingdom.

Before, During, and After Walt Disney Imagineering (WDI), which designs all of the parks, rides, and shows at Disney, has created a successful pattern you will see repeated again and again during your visit. First the pre-show, then the show, and finally the post-show. On the monorail or ferry you have entered the Magic Kingdom's pre-show, and are being prepared to enter the Happiest Place on Earth.

It Ain't Heavy, It's My Backpack In a bow to the modern world since 9/11, you can expect to have your bags and backpacks searched as you enter the park. Disney does this as cheerfully as possible—those security guys are Cast Members too, after all. But it should make you think twice about carrying too much stuff with you. Who wants to carry a bunch of junk around all day in a theme park anyway? As you enter, turn right if you want to rent a stroller or a wheelchair. Go straight under the railway station and turn right if you want to rent a locker to unload some of that stuff you brought.

©Disney 2003   *The Seven Seas Lagoon*

Main Street USA In the early days at WDW, lots of people had their offices up on the second floor above **Main Street USA**. Nobody works up there anymore, but you can imagine how much fun it must have been to have had an office in a location like that. ("Just whistle, while you work …"). The names painted on the windows of some of those second-story offices are the names of some of the early Imagineers and other executives at Disney.

Now that you are inside the park, you should have received your map and your Times Guide & New Information sheet. If not, turn left as you reach Main Street and pick them up at Guest Relations in **City Hall**. Here you can also set up Priority Seating for lunch or dinner. If you want a sit-down meal, inside an air-conditioned room, where someone waits on you (which will sound more and more attractive as the day goes on in spite of the premium price), take care of this before you do anything else. Above you, as you enter the park, is the platform for the **Walt Disney World Railroad**. The WDWRR is a genuine steam-powered railroad with engines built by Baldwin Locomotive Works in the early part of the 20th century. Disney found four of these locomotives being operated by the United Railways of Yucatan, had them dismantled,

©Disney 2003   *Main Street USA*

shipped to Tampa, and restored. They now run a route from **Main Street USA**, to **Frontierland**, to **Mickey's Toontown Fair**, and back again, and the railroad is Underutilized, as a rule. You may get tired later in the day, and if you do, remember that you can walk over to Frontierland or Toontown and hop a ride on the WDWRR back to the front of the park. The Main Street USA **Town Square** is the scene of many Character Greetings throughout the day. Check your Times Guide & New Information sheet for details.

DINING ON MAIN STREET USA

Tony's Town Square Restaurant, *and **The Plaza***
Table Service for lunch and dinner

Crystal Palace
Table Service for breakfast, lunch, and dinner

Casey's Corner, Main Street Bake Shop, Plaza Ice Cream Parlor
Quick Service and snacks

Assuming you haven't already taken the WDWRR to Frontierland or Mickey's Toontown Fair, early in the day you will probably want to blast past the shopping and dining on Main Street and walk toward Cinderella Castle. At the end of Main Street, on your left at the base of the castle, is a handy **Guest Information Board**.

This is a good place to stop, take a few pictures of the castle (mandatory activity), and plan an emergency rendezvous point. People do get separated in the Happiest Place on Earth.

Mapping It Out   This is the smallest of the WDW parks and the easiest to navigate. It is a circle with the seven Magic Kingdom lands located at compass points on the circle. The Cinderella Castle is in the center. You can move clockwise, counterclockwise, or randomly about the park, crossing back and forth through the castle. WDW research says that most people reach the castle, turn right, and move counterclockwise around the park. Consider doing the opposite, and you might find the

©Disney 2003
You must have your picture taken with Cinderella Castle. (It's in the rules.)

crowds smaller and the lines shorter as you head in the opposite direction from the majority of Guests. Theoretically speaking.

ADVENTURELAND

The best ride in this land is the **Jungle Cruise**, designed to Walt Disney's specifications for the opening of Disneyland in California in 1955. It is corny, punny, and after almost 50 years, it continues to entertain. It is also the most popular ride in Adventureland, so use FASTPASS if the line is long. There is much to do while you wait your turn. Walk over to the **Swiss Family Treehouse** for a minute. *The Swiss*

©Disney 2003

Magic Carpets of Aladdin

Family Robinson is a novel published in 1812-1813 by Johann David Wyss about a family marooned on an island. Though the modern reader might find the family's chronic cheerfulness a bit wearing, Disney nevertheless turned the story into a very likable movie in 1960, starring John Mills, Dorothy McGuire, and Tommy Kirk. This treehouse—in a faux Banyan—is modeled on the family's ingenious designs. It's a walk-through, so there shouldn't be a wait. **Pirates of the Caribbean** is almost as popular as the Jungle Cruise. It is a very simple ride, but its best feature may be that its line is almost entirely inside, where there is the benefit of air-conditioning. Installed in 1973, but envisioned by Walt

himself in the 1960s, it is most interesting for young children. The little boy in the boat ahead of me on a recent visit was worried that it might be too scary, but it grew on him. Small visitors will especially like the new ride, the **Magic Carpets of Aladdin**. Opened in May 2001, the MC of A is very similar to Dumbo the Flying Elephant in Fantasyland—with a few funny added bonuses. There are 16 carpets here with room for four Guests "on" each carpet.

DINING IN ADVENTURELAND

Aloha Isle, El Pirata Y el Perico,
Sunshine Tree Terrace
Quick Service and snacks

Finally, the **Enchanted Tiki Room–Under New Management** is a good time-filler. The original show opened with the park in 1971, but the Tiki birds go back further than that: they were among Walt Disney's first Audio-Animatronic designs. In 1998, the show was updated to include the "new man- agement" of Iago and

©Disney 2003

Pirates of the Caribbean

Zazu. The good news is that they still start the show with the Tiki-tiki-tiki-tiki-tiki song. This 9-minute experience is generally Underutilized and is always a great place to sit down.

FRONTIERLAND

Two of the best rides in the park are found in Frontierland. If you are not a sys- tematic person and your plan allows for hit-and-run fun, I would advise you to head for Frontierland first and then visit the other lands. **Splash Mountain** is the best ride in the park, in my opinion, and if you get here first thing on a not-too- crowded morning, you can sometimes ride it twice before the lines get too long. It is a roller coaster that plunges—at its peak—five stories into a stream at the bot- tom, and to much laughter, gets you good and wet. (You won't get nearly as wet here as you will on similar rides at Universal Studios Islands of Adventure. More about that in the Universal section.) If you have a delicate "do," it might not be your thing, but there is a good viewing area for the nonriders. The entire attrac- tion is themed to Disney's animated feature, *Song of the South*, and the "Zip-a- Dee-Doo-Dah" music is also a smile inducer. FASTPASS available. For the safety of the smallest park Guests, the Minimum Height Requirement on this ride is 40"/102 cm. (From now on we'll refer to this as the MHR.) The other top

---

DINING IN FRONTIERLAND

Aunt Polly's Dockside Inn, Diamond Horseshoe Saloon Revue,
Pecos Bill Café
Quick Service and snacks

Splash Mountain

attraction is **Big Thunder Mountain Railroad**. At 197 feet (60 meters) in height, it is claimed by WDW marketers to be the highest "mountain" in Florida. You should remind yourself to look around when you get to the top, because you get an excellent view of the entire park from up there. It is very likely, however, that you will be too busy holding on for dear life to remember to do so. When the line is long, this ride feels awfully short. FASTPASS available. MHR 40"/102 cm. The other activities in Frontierland are things you can do if you need to wait for your FAST-PASS reservation window. The best is **Tom Sawyer Island**. You take a raft to this little island, and on the way over you can give the little ones a brief synopsis of Mark Twain's *The Adventures of Tom Sawyer*, published in 1876. (Cliff's Notes version: Tom and his friend Huckleberry Finn get into and out of a lot of trouble, get lost in a cave, bad guy Injun Joe dies, and his treasure is divided between Tom and Huck.) On the island, there are suspension bridges and a fort to play on. Parents can watch and relax at *Aunt Polly's Dockside Inn*. Just remember: the island closes at dusk. The **Country Bear Jamboree** opened in 1971 at WDW and was later copied at Disneyland in Anaheim. It is as corny as Kansas in August. The **Frontierland Shootin' Arcade** began life as the Frontierland Shooting Gallery for the 1971 MK opening. Parents, take note: there is an additional cost here.

LIBERTY SQUARE

Walt Disney was a patriotic man, and Liberty Square is a tribute to feelings he hoped to share. The **Liberty Belle Riverboat** is a ride that pays tribute to the strength and beauty of America's waterways. The Liberty Belle is a genuine paddle-wheel steamer, but it runs on tracks, which you don't see as they are under water. The ride is 17 minutes long, one of the longest in the MK. "Mark Twain" hosts and provides the narration. A lot of Guests just walk by the **Hall of Presidents**, and they really should

stop and go in. The show here is inspiring for Americans and interesting as well for non-Americans curious about the American story. With each new presidential election, a new character—and I mean that in the nicest way—is added to the attraction. I've left the best for last: the **Haunted Mansion**. It is the most popular attraction in Liberty Square. It has nothing to do with liberty, but the illusions are excellent as ghosts come and go and the walls and ceilings appear to move in on you. I think it is pretty mild stuff, but it might be a little too intense for the tiniest of children. The 8-minute length is very satisfying. FASTPASS is available to help circumvent the lines.

©Disney 2003
George W. Bush recently joined the Hall of Presidents

DINING IN LIBERTY SQUARE

Liberty Tree Tavern
Table Service for lunch and dinner

Columbia Harbour House, Sleepy Hollow
Quick Service and snacks

FANTASYLAND

. When most people think of the Walt Disney World Resort, this is the land that comes to mind. Tinkerbell, Dumbo, Peter Pan, Cinderella, and Pooh are all here. All the rides are enjoyable for both children and adults, and because of that, there can be considerable wait times.

One of the most popular attractions here is the **Many Adventures of Winnie the Pooh**, an addition installed in 1999. Pooh and friends became part of the Disney stable when Walt Disney himself signed a contract to merchandise them in the United States in 1961. These A. A. Milne characters are now Disney's most popular merchandise assets, worth about 1 billion dollars in annual revenue, according to *Fortune*

©Disney 2003

Magazine, January 6, 2003. There was some grousing from diehard Disneyphiles when Pooh replaced Mr. Toad's Wild Ride, but now this three-and-a-half-minute ride-in-a-honey-pot is one of the park's most popular, and is a FASTPASS ride. Note to stock watchers: there has been an ongoing legal struggle over the rights to these Milne characters. Check on details if you are interested in investing.

Peter Pan's Flight is said to have been Walt Disney's favorite ride—when it opened in Anaheim in 1955. This flight in a pirate ship above Never Never Land and Victorian London remains very popular today. It also has FASTPASS. **Snow White's Scary Adventures** is another oldie-but-goodie. The witch who appears in this attraction can prove to be a bit frightening but, that's just a tribute to Disney artistry. Based on the 1937 Disney animated classic, *Snow White and the Seven Dwarfs*, it may make you want to go home and see the movie again. Tucked amongst all these rides is a new show in Fantasyland. **Mickey's PhilharMagic**

<hr>

DINING IN FANTASYLAND

Cinderella's Royal Table
Table Service, Priority Seating recommended for breakfast, lunch, and dinner

Enchanted Grove, Mrs. Potts' Cupboard, Pinocchio Village Haus, Scuttle's Landing
Quick Service and snacks

(debut October 2003) is a mix of 3-D film with live action and sound. Designed for the whole family, it has been installed in the hall that most recently hosted the Legend of the Lion King. Before that (1971-1980) it was home to the Mickey Mouse Revue. This is a FASTPASS attraction. The ride with the most history in this part of the park is **it's a small world**, a ride that encompasses a world *so small* that Disney's has eliminated all capital letters from the ride's name! Walt Disney designed this 10-minute boat ride for the 1964 World's Fair in New York. Its optimistic look at the global village appears just a tad over the top today, but the song is infectious. You'll be singing it the rest of the day. WDW calls this "The Happiest Cruise That Ever Sailed"—a slogan the marketers cooked up long before the Disney Cruise Line docked in Port Canaveral.

©Disney 2003   *Cinderella's Golden Carrousel*

Dumbo the Flying Elephant is a simple carnival ride themed so beautifully that its picture has been seen around the world. The cars used to be smaller, but the ride became so popular that the old cars were retired and larger ones were created to accommodate more passengers. The cars are painted in an old-fashioned circus color scheme of mostly primary tones, and the little elephant with the big ears looks so happy, you feel as if you would like to join him aloft. The 2-minute ride has a very low Throughput, so there is almost always a line. Ditto for the **Mad Tea Party**, another ride on the most-photographed list. This ride has a simple design, simply executed. The teacups are great fun to ride—unless spinning turns you green.

Cinderella's Golden Carrousel is a genuine old-fashioned carrousel. Built for the Detroit Palace Garden Park in 1917, it was later moved to Maplewood Olympic

Park in New Jersey. Imagineers discovered and refurbished it for Fantasyland and most of the carrousel animals are no longer the originals. It is worth a ride just to take the time to enjoy its beauty. Finally, there is **Ariel's Grotto**, where Ariel the Little Mermaid greets Guests for pictures and autographs here in a little spot behind Dumbo. (She doesn't walk well on those fins so you need to go to her.)

©Disney 2003

The Barnstormer

Mickey's Toontown Fair This special park-within-a-park began life as Mickey's Birthdayland, became Mickey's Starland in 1988, and was transformed into Mickey's Toontown Fair in 1996. It is designed for little ones, and since they generally tire out early in the day, if you come later in the day you'll find it less crowded. (But will your children be awake? Hmm.) It includes **Mickey's Country House** and **Minnie's Country House**, where you will learn the secret of Mickey and Minnie's relationship. They are neighbors, of course. Each of them has a pint-sized home here that is a playground for little Guests. The **Toontown Hall of Fame Tent** is both a show and a shop as well as a place to meet and greet a range of Disney characters—other than Mickey. Signs let you know who is on hand. The **Judge's Tent** is the place to go when you and your family want to have a meeting with the Big Guy—Mickey Mouse himself. He'll pose for pictures and give you his John Hancock. To say this is a popular spot is an understatement. **Donald's Boat** is a lot like your little ones—it leaks like a sieve. In this case, it is all in fun. The **Barnstormer at Goofy's Wiseacre Farm** is a miniature roller coaster for children. It is not too scary, but the MHR is 35"/89 cm.

TOMORROWLAND

Tomorrowland struggled for a while as the world of tomorrow came upon us so quickly that it became impossible for fantasy to keep pace with reality. When Imagineers finally figured out that Tomorrowland didn't have to be about a *real* vision of the future, things began to gel again in this land.

> One note: two attractions in Tomorrowland may not be open when you visit: **Carousel of Progress** and the **Timekeeper**. Check your Times Guide & New Information sheet for details.

Space Mountain is a Tomorrowland hot ticket. At 180 feet (55 meters) high, this is almost-but-not-quite as tall as Cinderella Castle. Added to Tomorrowland in 1975, it was "flight tested" by U.S. astronauts and Russian cosmonauts—back when getting the two together was pretty unusual. Depending on the lines, it can take awhile to get to the top of the "mountain," but it won't take you any time at all to come down. FASTPASS reduces wait times. It is labeled too intense for children and some adults. MHR is 44"/112 cm. The other two popular rides in Tomorrowland are **Buzz Lightyear's Space Ranger Spin** and **The ExtraTERRORestrial Alien Encounter**. Buzz opened in 1998 on the heels of the success of the movie *Toy Story*. Buzz has a heart of gold, but as we all know he takes himself pretty seriously, and that naturally makes him a very funny guy. Great show, no restrictions. FASTPASS available. Alien is scary. In fact, rumor had it that when this was being test-ed, prior to opening in 1995, Disney bosses asked that it be toned down a notch because it was feared to be TOO SCARY. Was it changed or not? Was the rumor even true?

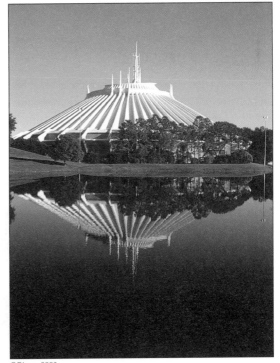

©Disney 2003

Space Mountain

DINING IN TOMORROWLAND

Auntie Gravity's Galactic Goodies, Cosmic Ray's Starlight Café, Lunching Pad, Plaza Pavilion
Quick Service and snacks

Judge for yourself. FAST-PASS available. MHR is 44"/112 cm. A couple of classics remain in Tomorrowland to help you fill time. They include **Astro Orbiter**, which is yet another version of the Dumbo ride. It too has a low Throughput, so they keep the ride to just 2 minutes in length. **Tomorrowland Transit Authority** was originally called the WEDway People Mover when it was installed in 1975. (WED was the original acronym for Disney's design department—now called Walt Disney Imagineering or WDI). It takes you on a route over Tomorrowland, and there is almost never a line. The shade up there is pretty nice too. During the busiest seasons, the **Tomorrowland Stage** and the **Galaxy Palace Theater** have live entertainment. Check your Times Guide & New Information sheet for details. Finally, the **Tomorrowland Indy Speedway** is the ride that was once just the plain old Tomorrowland Speedway, which itself was a re-do of the old Autopia ride in Disneyland. Whatever you call the ride, kids love the chance it gives them to "drive" a "real" car, and why not? If *you* could just abandon *your* car at the end of the day and walk away from it, you'd enjoy driving too! MHR to ride alone is 52"/132 cm.

That's the basic rundown on the Magic Kingdom. If you've made one loop and still have some energy remaining, check the daily schedule for the parade, fireworks, and Character Greeting times. Otherwise, remember that you are on vacation and are allowed to return to the hotel pool at any time without fear of being thrown in vacation jail for not exhausting yourself completely.

Astro Orbiter

©Disney 2003

CINDERELLA CASTLE

The Cinderella Castle is the central icon or symbol of the Magic Kingdom, just as Sleeping Beauty Castle is the central icon of Disneyland, in California. Cinderella Castle is 190 feet tall, and the flagpole on its highest tower makes it the tallest structure in the Magic Kingdom. The forced perspective (things are painted to look smaller, the higher they get) used in the design causes the structure to appear to be about one hundred feet taller than its actual height.

There is no real castle quite like it. Designers looked at medieval castles in France and the Rhine Valley, but they used their imaginations to design this one. It sits atop a series of tunnels created so Cast Members working in the Magic Kingdom can enter and leave their stations via elevators, without having to cross through Fantasyland, for example, wearing a Tomorrowland costume. The tunnels are also used for dressing rooms, supplies, storage, offices and to help remove refuse without interfering with the enjoyment of Guests. The tunnels were somewhat of a secret for many years, but in 1996, Walt Disney World allowed them to be shown on Oprah Winfrey's television program, so I'm not giving anything away.

Although the building appears to be built of large stone blocks, it is actually made of fiberglass. An apartment was built inside the castle for the Disney family, but it was never completed and has never been used. The castle's only full-time resident is Tinkerbell, who flies down each night to announce that it is time for the fireworks to begin.

THE ABSOLUTELY ESSENTIAL EPCOT

Festivals Epcot has two of the best festivals at WDW. The first is the Epcot International Flower and Garden Festival, and the second is the Epcot International Food and Wine Festival. Both are worth planning a vacation around.

The Epcot International Flower and Garden Festival This takes place annually in the spring for about six weeks, generally in May and June. Disney Horticulture really puts on a show, with topiary, orchid gardens, giant butterflies, water gardens, even gardens planted all in food crops in the Land pavilion. In recent years, the festival has added live performances by rock and roll groups from the 1960s and 1970s—under the theme "flower power"—as well as art and sculpture from around the world. There is an ongoing schedule of gardening and flower-arranging demonstrations and a special line of merchandise. They even fly in roses from Ecuador for Mother's Day.

©Disney 2003
The Food and Wine Festival is Epcot's biggest event.

The International Food and Wine Festival This started small, with one part-time organizer, and has become Epcot's biggest draw. It is held annually in the autumn for about five weeks, beginning early in October. Every well-known vineyard—from France, Chile, Australia, Argentina, California, Italy, and more—sends top representatives to this festival for wine-tastings and demonstrations. Internationally known chefs take part in a schedule of culinary classes and tastings. Once again, there is special merchandise unique to each year. Small stands are added to the World Showcase Promenade, where you can taste quick bites (and lovely sips) from around the world.

Holidays The holiday season is not short on celebrations throughout WDW, but Epcot puts on a very popular holiday festival of its own with its evening

Candlelight event and Holidays Around the World. This politically correct festival salutes all the winter holidays from Hanukkah to Kwanza to Christmas and features a different choir each night (generally school groups, some Disney pros, and some Disney volunteers) singing medleys of traditional holiday songs. The show also features a Broadway-caliber star who serves as narrator. A dinner package is available for an extra charge, which provides Priority Seating at an Epcot restaurant and reserved seating at the show.

Schedules For information on the dates of the Epcot International Flower and Garden Festival, the Epcot International Food and Wine Festival, and Holidays Around the World, call **407-824-4321** or log on to www.disney-world.com.

©Disney 2003

Pin Trading This idea began at Epcot during the Millennium Celebration and spread to all the Disney parks and attractions. I don't know if people actually trade these pins, but they definitely collect them, and Epcot merchandise obliges by issuing limited edition pins for each season, festival, Disney anniversary, and event. Many collectors wear their pins on lanyards around their necks or pinned to their hats. Because of Epcot's international themes, it seems to have the richest variety of pins.

Parlez Vous? The Cast Members within Epcot's World Showcase, are recruited from the 11 nations represented by pavilions. The young people stay together in Disney apartment complexes, where friendships and romances take on a truly international flavor. They get to stay only for a year. Their name tags will tell you where they come from, and you will find they love to talk about home and about the experiences they are having in the United States. These young people are Epcot's greatest asset. If you know someone from one of the World Showcase countries who would like to work at Epcot, call International Programs at **407-934-7470** or **407-828-1000**.

©Disney 2003　*The hand of Sorcerer Mickey and the wand were added to Epcot's geodesic sphere for the Millennium Celebration. Originally topped with "2000," the numbers were later removed and replaced with the Epcot logo.*

The Park of Discovery

EPCOT

The layout of Epcot is that of a world's fair. Just as world's fairs do, Epcot has an area where new ideas and new technologies are displayed—**Future World**—and an area where world cultures are explored—**World Showcase**. The park opened just about the time that world's fairs were losing their clout; so since about the mid-1990s, Epcot managers, fearing the deflation in world's fair caché may hurt the park, have worked hard to add to the park's attractions. Epcot is laid out in the shape of a large figure eight, with Future World at the bottom of the eight, and World Showcase along the top. The liveliest things to see and do are in Future World. The best places to shop and eat are in World Showcase. The park is 300 acres—the World Showcase Promenade alone is about a mile in length—so you'll want to pace yourself. On average, Epcot has about one-half to one-third as much attendance as the Magic Kingdom; there are fewer crowds to jostle you, but a lot more walking.

Spaceship Earth–Open for Business　Epcot usually opens an hour later than the Magic Kingdom, but that is subject to change, so call **407-824-4321**, or log on to www.disneyworld.com to be absolutely certain. When you enter the park through the front gates, you enter Future World. Since it takes time for people to move through Future World, World Showcase opens one to two hours later than the front gates of the park.

Stop, in the Name of Epcot Driving in, you stop at the Epcot tollgate to pay for parking. Prices vary depending on whether you are driving a school bus or your family wagon. (See the entrance and parking information on the MK.)

Put 'Er There At Epcot, once you park your car, you are there. Most of the time you can park close enough not to need to take the tram, though trams run all day for those parked farthest away. Remember a) to lock your car, b) not to leave anything in it that can be ruined by heat, and c) to make a note of where you parked. The Epcot parking lot is so big that at certain times of the year Epcot Special Events puts up tents and hosts entire conventions in its vast reaches.

Tickets If you have bought your tickets or you have one of the Park Hopper tickets, you can head right in. Otherwise, you can buy tickets adjacent to the Epcot Entrance Plaza.

NO BREAD CRUMBS NECESSARY
Remember: you cannot get lost on the Walt Disney World roads (please don't prove me wrong on this). All roads and all signs lead to the parks. If you are on I-4, take Exit 65. If you are staying On Property, take the monorail or buses provided free to hotel guests. From the Swan, Dolphin, Yacht and Beach, and BoardWalk resorts, you can walk or take a water launch to Epcot's International Gateway. This entrance is at the World Showcase bridge between the United Kingdom and France. Your hotel will very likely also have shuttle service available.

The Look Epcot's Entrance Plaza has a look that is different from any other Disney theme park anywhere. It is bold, gray, and almost stark, and rising above it is the Epcot symbol—the huge silver sphere called Spaceship Earth. This is the pre-show. It is announcing to you a very different experience from the warm, and fuzzy, Magic Kingdom. This simple, broad setting has turned out to be a very beautiful canvas for the work of WDW Horticulture. Here, the landscaping is an integral part of the show.

Leave a Legacy As you cross the plaza you will notice a group of large cement stalagmites on either side of you. These are holdovers from the Millennium Celebration and are called "Leave a Legacy." Guests can have their photographs taken and turned into etched tiles that are placed on these free-form pieces of sculpture. Ask at the adjacent kiosk for more information.

Future World There are ten pavilions here with an eleventh pavilion—Odyssey—that is now used for special events. As you enter the park, you first see **Spaceship Earth**, and going clockwise from your left are the **Universe of Energy**, the **Wonders of Life**, **Mission: Space**, **Test Track**, **Odyssey**, **Imagination**, the **Land**, and the **Living Seas**. In the center are **Innoventions East** and **Innoventions West**.

> **Dining** Epcot has the best food at WDW. In Future World there are two Table Service restaurants: *Coral Reef* and *Garden Grill*. *Coral Reef* sits on the edge of the Living Seas, where you can dine on fish and shellfish while you watch their cousins cavort in one of the world's largest man-made aquariums. *Garden Grill*, in the Land pavilion, is as bright and sunny as *Coral Reef* is softly lit and mysterious. Both have first-rate gourmet menus and Priority Seating is recommended. Both are open for lunch and dinner only.

Simpler Fare in Future World: *Electric Umbrella* is on Innoventions Plaza; *Fountain View Espresso and Bakery* is across the plaza from the *Electric Umbrella* and has coffee and sweets. *Pure and Simple* is in the Wonders of Life pavilion and has good food disguised as healthy food; *Sunshine Season Food Fair* in the Land is like one of those food pavilions at the local mall. These all offer Quick Service and snacks.

©Disney 2003

Be sure you're hungry when you visit Epcot. The food is great.

Future World Is So Big! What Do You Do First? Come early for the best experience. As is true at the Magic Kingdom, the front gates of the park often open before the attractions do, so you can get a morning snack and get oriented. Then, if you haven't yet made Priority Seating plans for lunch or dinner, do that now, at Guest Relations adjacent to Spaceship Earth, or at the tip board on the plaza as you enter. Before you arrive or from your cell phone you can call **407-WDW-Dine (407-939-3463)** for Priority Seating. Once that is done, I would head to the three

©Disney 2003

Lightning can close Test Track, so go in the morning.

hot tickets for a ride, a FASTPASS reservation, or queuing. **Test Track, Mission: Space,** and **Honey, I Shrunk the Audience** are the three top rides in Future World. Once you get those checked off your list, you can relax and enjoy the rest of the day.

The first attraction you will see as you enter Future World is **Spaceship Earth**, and it has a slow but enjoyable ride inside. It is a journey through the history of communications in a car disguised as a time machine. You go up into the sphere, and at the top feel your car turn sideways so you can see the genuine spaceship earth projected onto an image of a huge sky. This ride is nice, but it isn't a "must-see" so if it is crowded, you can move on.

©Disney 2003

Mission Space debuted October 2003.

In the center of the plaza ahead you will find **Innoventions East** and **West**. This piece of Epcot was created as an up-to-the-minute technology show. The exhibits are commercial, it is true. But that gives these companies a very good place to test some of their new ideas on consumers, and in turn, it gives Epcot's Guests a chance to see things before everybody else does. Exhibits are organized as exits on the Road to Tomorrow and have as their host a little robot called Tom Morrow 2.0. I would save Innoventions for later in the day when you've done the rest of the park and would like to spend some time inside an air-conditioned pavilion.

To the left of Spaceship Earth is the **Universe of Energy**. The entire experience takes 45 minutes, which is quite a contrast to the 2-and 3-minute attractions over in the Magic Kingdom. It includes a ride as well as a movie, starring (former ABC star) Ellen DeGeneris as well as Bill Nye the Science Guy, and (most popular among kids) some Audio-Animatronic dinosaurs. Ask a Cast Member how much time is left until the next show and how many in the line will make it in before you commit. If you ask these questions it will help you decide whether to wait or come back later.

Moving clockwise around the park, the next pavilion you'll come to is **Wonders of Life**. There are several hours of activities within this pavilion, set up under the theme "Fitness Fairgrounds." Self-guided attractions are the **Wonder Cycles**,

Sensory Funhouse, **Lifestyle Review** (where you probably shouldn't reveal the diet-busting you're doing at Epcot), and **Frontiers of Medicine**. More structured attractions include **Goofy About Health**, **The Making of Me**, and **Cranium Command**. The most popular attraction in the pavilion is **Body Wars**, a homage to the film *Fantastic Voyage* (1966), in which some scientists are made really small and injected into a body. To simulate this experience, the seats in this show rock and roll quite a bit. People who tend to motion sickness should probably pass. The Minimum Height Requirement (MHR) for Body Wars is 40"/102 cm. (This pavilion is closed from time to time, so just move on if it is.) As you continue clockwise around Future World, you'll reach **Mission: Space**, constructed between 2000 and 2003 on the site of the old Horizons pavilion.

> **Mission: Space** is the first new E-ticket at Epcot since Test Track in 1999. It is an experience designed to make you feel as if you really have been into space, from g-forces to weightlessness. I used to enjoy being rocked to sleep in those chairs inside the darkness of Horizons; this attraction will definitely not have that effect on you.

©Disney 2003
The old Horizons pavilion was demolished and Mission Space was built in its place.

Next to Mission: Space is Epcot's other thrill ride, **Test Track**. Retrofitted into the old World of Motion pavilion, Test Track became Epcot's first thrill ride in 1999. Everyone who visits the park wants to ride it, which, for a while, meant some long wait times. Now, you can use FASTPASS. In the summer be sure to experience this ride early in the day. Lightning, which often strikes in the afternoon in Florida, can close the attraction. There is a singles line to your far left as you face the attraction, and it is almost always a speedy way to go, though children under age seven are prohibited from using it. The ride goes out over the Epcot backstage area, but you are going so fast (65 mph at one point), I'll bet you can't see it. The MHR is 40"/102 cm.

Ice Station Cool (a detour) Between Test Track and Imagination as you go clock-wise around Future World, you will cross Showcase Plaza. If you are feeling warm, you might want to duck (forgive me, Donald) into **Ice Station Cool**, right on the edge of Innoventions West, as you walk toward Imagination. It snows here 365 days a year, and you don't have to shovel any of it. You can sample eight differ-ent soft drinks from around the world (small cups, no charge). Built as part of Disney's deal with Coca-Cola, there is an array of Coca-Cola logo merchandise for sale. Between Innoventions East and Innoventions West is another cooler-off-er: the **Fountain of Nations**. It is programmed to put on a performance to music every fifteen minutes. If you stand close enough to it during show time, you'll not only catch a good show, you'll catch some of the fountain's mist that is carried on the breeze.

©Disney 2003

"Honey" is a hit at "Imag."

Now you'll probably want to head over to the pavilion called **Imagination**. Thrill-ride schmill-ride: I say "Imag" (pronounced Eye-Madge) contains the one must-see at Epcot. **Honey, I Shrunk The Audience** is funny and creative and includes lots of surprises. The pre-show photomontage is thoughtful, artistic, and a great blood pressure reducer. You can now use FASTPASS on Honey, and there is another attraction—**Journey into Imagination with Figment**—to enjoy while you wait. Figment is the only character unique to Epcot—he appears nowhere else at Disney—and the little purple dragon is extremely popular. When Imagineers redesigned the ride in 1999, they barely included old Figment and there was a hue and cry from Figmentistas. The re-re-done ride assuaged concerns, and Figment is now, once again, a featured player. The song "One Little Spark" is also back on the Journey and the whole thing spills out into the **Imageworks "What If" Labs**.

The pavilion next to Imag is the **Land**. Spanning six acres, all indoors, this is the largest pavilion at Epcot. It contains three attractions: **Food Rocks**, a 15-minute show that little kids really like; **Circle of Life**, a 20-minute eco-film featuring some well-known stars of Disney animation; and **Living with the Land**, a 14-minute boat ride that takes you through a range of environments and ecosystems and ends in probably the most amazing garden you'll ever see. Here and out behind this attraction in the Epcot greenhouses, Epcot grows 30 tons of fruits and vegetables, many of them used in the Epcot restaurants. The Land, under the aegis of Epcot Director of Science Dr. Fred Petitt, also works with NASA, the World Bank, and the U.S. Department of Agriculture on experiments designed to find new ways to feed the world's hungry, which shows that the spirit of Walt Disney's Experimental Prototype Community of Tomorrow really is alive and well here. Living with the Land now has FAST-PASS, and there are no size restrictions for riders.

If you want to learn more about the real work being done at the Land, you can take a one-hour guided tour called **Behind the Seeds**. Call **407-939-8687** to make reservations, or ask at the Green Thumb Emporium. There is a small charge.

The **Living Seas** has a great-looking exterior feature—that crash of surf that spouts through the rocks out front. Inside is a huge aquarium tank that holds 6 million

©Disney 2003
You can dive at the Living Seas, if you are certified.

gallons of water and is home to 2,000 marine creatures. The show, which is a teensy bit tired, includes a film and a trip to an "undersea research center," where at Sea Base Alpha, you can learn more about the marine denizens that swim all around you. The best thing about the attraction is the **Coral Reef Restaurant**, which I've already mentioned. All the tables are situated so guests face the tank. Only in large groups does this make communication among those at the table a challenge. Certified scuba divers might be interested in **DiveQuest**, which allows you to dive right into the tank. (When you are eating in the restaurant, it is always interesting to see someone swim by!) Another experience, **Dolphins in Depth**, is a backstage look at the pavilion's dolphin research. Call **407-WDW-Tour (407-939-8687)** to schedule.

©Disney 2003

World Showcase

World Showcase There are 11 nations in World Showcase and the experiences at each pavilion include authentic dining, shopping, and drinking. The rides and attractions on this side of the park are not as exciting as those in Future World, but by the time you arrive in World Showcase, perhaps you'll be ready to relax. On most days, World Showcase doesn't open until 11 a.m., so except on rare occasions (New Year's Eve for example, when all kinds of exceptions are made), none of the restaurants in World Showcase serves breakfast. Pastry and coffee are available in France, if you are really hungry, and even if you aren't, they still taste great. Look for the **KidCot Fun Stops**, which Epcot added so that little children could enjoy World Showcase too. Each Fun Stop is directed by an international Cast Member who directs children at tot-sized tables in mask-making and other playful activities.

It isn't difficult to spot **Mexico** with the Mayan pyramid rising above the promenade. Inside, there is an attraction called **El Rio Del Tiempo** (the River of Time) that takes you through the history of Mexico in a 6-minute boat ride. The pace is more that of a tramp steamer than a

©Disney 2003

speedboat. At the back of the pavilion, there is Table Service at the *San Angel Inn*. All the goods for sale here are products of Mexico, where Disney merchandise specialists go on frequent buying trips. Some Guests have been known to bend their elbows at the *Cantina de San Angel* on the promenade, where beer and margaritas are sold. Watch and listen for the Mariachi Cobre, a Mexican band in traditional costume.

Norway's dramatic landmark is the replica of a Stave Church. The Vikings built these old churches of wood in the early days of Norway's conversion to Christianity, and very few have survived. Inside this one is a rotating Norwegian cultural exhibit and

you'll find the space an oasis of serenity as you step in from the Florida sunlight. The table service restaurant in Norway, *Akershus*, has a buffet that really does taste like home cooking—if your Mom is a really good cook. The **Maelstrom** is the pavilion's main attraction, and since there are so few rides in World Showcase, it can attract a crowd, so FASTPASS is now available for it. Don't ask for a "Danish" at *Kringla Bakeri og Kafe*—but should you ask for a "Norwegian" instead? Hmm. Shopping opportunities here range from trolls to genuine Norwegian ski sweaters.

©Disney 2003

The two best things about the **China** pavilion are the Chinese acrobats, who perform on the promenade throughout the day, and the flat-out fabulous shopping at **Yong Feng Shangdian**. The operator of the pavilion is a Chinese American businessman, who brought his nephew over from Shanghai to handle the pavilion's day-to-day business. Both men travel frequently to China to acquire merchandise,

©Disney 2003

and if you shop carefully, you can find antiques and rare items here that will be difficult to find anywhere else in the United States. There is a film here called **Wonders of China** (Circle-Vision, 19 minutes, no seats). The Table Service restaurant, *Nine Dragons*, has a noodle maker who flings around dough that turns into Chinese noodles. Quite a show! Quicker bites—if you want to save time for shopping—are available at *Lotus Blossom Café*. The Chinese acrobats include some young people who appear to be able to fly, the way they do in those new Chinese movies.

In Epcot's **Germany**, there is nothing to do but eat, drink, shop, and be merry. For Table Service, there is *Biergarten*, at the rear of the pavilion, where the food is buffet style, the beer is Beck's, and the entertainment includes yodeling. *Sommerfest*, is a café with outside tables and Quick Service. Shopping here features porcelain by Hummel and Goebel, German Christmas ornaments, Rhine wines, jewelry, crystal, Teddy bears, and toys. Next door in **Italy**, you'll find one of the most popular Table Service restaurants in World Showcase. At *L'Originale Alfredo di Roma*, they make their own noodles, and many of them are served as Fettuccine Alfredo, the dish named after this restaurant's mother ship in Rome. Priority Seating is recommended. There are three places to shop here for Italian goods. Keep a lookout for the marble statues that move. They sometimes stroll along with you, and they aren't nearly as annoying as those mimes in San Francisco.

©Disney 2003

The American Adventure This is the America of idealism and optimism, from sea to shining sea. The attraction has a pre-show that features the Voices of Liberty and/or American Vybe, performing traditional American music. The show—in a beautiful, comfortable, upstairs theater—is a 26-minute filmed look at American history, with frequent interruptions by "Ben Franklin," "Thomas Jefferson," and "Mark Twain" (the Audio-Animatronic variety). Outside, those who have been walking the promenade craving American food, can satisfy their hunger at the **Liberty Inn** with Quick Service and nice places to sit both inside and out. The **American Gardens Theater** (known as AmGard) is the home of Holidays Around the World in December, classic rock and roll in the spring, and sometimes in the summer, Broadway-quality stage performances. Check your Times Guide & New Information sheet for details. As you face the attraction, look to your right. Horticulture has created a formal early American garden here worth a second look. If you bring your own snack, it provides a nice, shady place to sit with your family.

In **Japan**, the real shows are the Zen gardens and the historic Japanese architecture. They provide a contrast to the bustle of the **Mitsukoshi Department Store**, which is a small version of the stores Mitsukoshi owns in Japan. Did I mention that Mitsukoshi sponsors this pavilion? Japanese drummers entertain on the prome-

©Disney 2003

nade, and there are three places to eat. The two with Table Service are **Tempura Kiku**, which serves batter-fried foods, sushi, and sashimi, and **Teppanyaki Dining Rooms**, a Japanese steak house. I like the Quick Service at **Yakitori House**, because you can carry your tray to the tables right on the edge of the gardens. Next door you'll find **Morocco**. A friend from the Middle East stood and stared as we entered this pavilion because, he said, it looks exactly like the old parts of the city of Marrakesh. The reason it does is that the Kingdom of Morocco sent craftsmen to Epcot to tile all the mosaics here by hand. There is no ride in Morocco, but there are four places to shop and two places to eat. Stop at the Moroccan National Tourist Office if you would like a tour of the pavilion or information on a trip to, say, Casablanca. The Table Service restaurant, coincidentally called **Marrakesh**, is best known for the belly dancer who entertains here and who will often find a willing Guest to join her (to much snapping of pictures). I highly recommend the Quick Service at **Tangierine Café** (the name is a takeoff on the name of the city Tangiers, not the little orange fruit), where you will find authentic dishes like hummus, tabbouleh, pita, and lamb that you can mix and match for an excellent meal.

©Disney 2003

You can't miss **France** or its icon, the familiar Eiffel Tower (as opposed to the Earffel tower over at Disney MGM Studios). For an aerial view of the country, there is **Impressions de France**. It is an 18-minute film, shown on five screens, for a 200-degree view of French town and country, and it provokes the most oohs and ahs in World Showcase. There are five places to shop and three places to eat. The Epcot Veep I used to work for almost always scheduled our business lunches at **Les Chefs de France**, and I think you should take that as an endorsement, since he was a very fastidious person. At *Chefs*, Table Service is available for lunch and dinner, and you should definitely schedule Priority Seating. The restaurant building was enlarged in 1998, and it now features **Bistro de Paris** (dinner only, not always open) on the second floor. **Boulangerie Patisserie** is a small Quick Service café. The French flower garden looks like something out of an Impressionist painting—another example of WDW Horticulture doing a great job. Beyond the garden, at the edge of France, you will often find appearances by Disney characters with French roots, such as Belle from *Beauty and the Beast*.

As you continue clockwise around World Showcase you'll cross the bridge between France and the United Kingdom. If you were to turn left after you crossed the bridge, you would reach **International Gateway**. This is what you might call a back door to Epcot, the only entrance of its kind in all the WDW parks. You can walk to this entrance from the Swan, Dolphin, Yacht and Beach Club, and the BoardWalk, and if you want to visit only World Showcase this is a great way to enter. If you feel like taking a break from the park, you can also exit here, walk to one of the resorts for lunch or dinner and return, if you remember to get your hand stamped before you leave the park.

Are you full of international cuisine and laden with packages? Hang on to your bonnet: the **United Kingdom** is the next stop for shopping and eating. This pavilion is also known for a band called the British Invasion, which plays on a regular schedule in the square and sounds and looks suspiciously like the Beatles. If you plan ahead and schedule Priority Seating for the **Rose and Crown**, this little pub on the edge of the World Showcase Lagoon is a great place to end your evening watching Epcot's closing fireworks show, **IllumiNations**. Don't forget to request an outside table. Moving on from there it's shop, shop, shop. Royal Doulton, tartans, British toys, cashmere sweaters—all the best of British imports are for sale in the United Kingdom. Somehow, WDW Horticulture keeps the gardens in the U.K. looking like genuine English perennial borders, in spite of Florida's subtropical climate.

Next door to the U.K. is the Commonwealth of **Canada**. Cast Members wear black and red lumberjack shirts, and they always make me think of that Monty Python song ("I'm a Lumberjack, and I'm Okay"), but maybe one just gets punchy after all the cultural stimulation of one's cruise around World Showcase. Canada has a

Circle-Vision show called **O Canada**, which takes you on a 17-minute visit to North America's northerly nation. You need to be able to turn to see all parts of the screen, so just as in China, there aren't any seats for this show. The totem pole you see in this pavilion is not a set piece: a native from one of Canada's indigenous tribes spent a year at Epcot carving it. The Table Service restaurant, *Le Cellier*, has won award after award for excellence, so call ahead for Priority Seating. This restaurant's only negative is that it doesn't have a view, even though it sits right next to the pavilion's rose garden. Still, even as I say this, I can hear Epcot's

©Disney 2003

French-speaking Executive Chef, my friend and former office-mate Michael Pythoud, telling me rather sternly that Le Cellier means "the cellar" in French, so OF COURSE IT DOESN'T HAVE WINDOWS! For entertainment, look for Off Kilter, a rock band in kilts. No whistling now, ladies.

That is a complete circuit of both Future World and World Showcase. Yet Epcot has one more offering that makes it a very popular place to end the day. **IllumiNations: Reflections of Earth** closes the evening with a history of Planet Earth in 13 minutes; but that is a much-too-blasé description of a show that includes more than 1,100 fireworks shells, lasers, and an earth globe that appears to float in out of nowhere. This is the third incarnation of IllumiNations at Epcot, and it is not likely to be the last. Check your Times Guide & New Information sheet for the latest.

THE ABSOLUTELY ESSENTIAL DISNEY-MGM STUDIOS

Parades and Fireworks There is a daily parade at the Disney-MGM Studios (almost always based on a Disney movie) that takes place about mid-day, but this, as with all entertainment, is subject to change. Fireworks are presented at the end of the day, but not every day. For information on both, check your Times Guide & New Information sheet or ask any Cast Member.

ABC Super Soaps Weekend For one weekend in November, fans get a chance to see the stars of their favorite soaps. Quite often there are stars visiting WDW on other days, but you won't be able to know about these visits until you are

©Disney 2003

You can check in, but can you check out?

Nostalgia for old Hollywood is what Disney-MGM Studios is all about. There is some genuine movie memorabilia for sale at The Studios, but you won't find this vintage postcard folder for sale there. It belongs to me!

in the park. They are an added bonus for Guests. Check the website at www.disneyworld.com for dates and times of Super Soaps Weekend and other special events.

Osborne Family Festival of Lights Jennings Osborne (no relation to Ozzie) and his family got nationwide coverage of the enormous number of Christmas lights they were using each year to decorate their Arkansas home. Disney decided relocate the show to Disney MGM Studios. The display now includes 5 milli lights, and though everything you see at WDW is first rate, this is, in WDW pa ance, a "wow." This show is on hiatus for the 2003 holiday season, but i expected to come back in 2004. Ask Cast Members if you have any questic It generally runs late November through the New Year.

Star Wars Weekends For about five weeks in late May and early June, the Wars characters appear on weekends to make sure the Force Is with You. is a rare, rare, rare, example of non-Disney characters appearing in a Di park, and it's definitely worth coming to see.

The Twilight Zone™ is a registered trademark of CBS, Inc. and is used pursuant to a license from CBS, Inc.　©Disney 2003

Sunset Boulevard at the Disney-MGM Studios.

Action!
DISNEY-MGM STUDIOS

The Studios (as it is called inside WDW) was the third park built at Walt Disney World, and it provides an experience that is very different, in many ways, from those at the first two parks. It is not the kind of place in which it will be especially productive for you to wander around, choosing your adventures as you go. The paths through the park have several dead ends from which you cannot access other areas. Nearly half of the attractions are shows, and they operate on a posted schedule. Finally, Disney-MGM Studios has about half the number of attractions of the Magic Kingdom. The attractions are, on average, longer experiences, so the pace is different here. The wisest thing to do at The Studios is to get a park map and a Times Guide & New Information sheet when you first arrive, sit down for a minute, and plan your day.

Saddle Your Ponies By now you are probably getting a little bit more comfortable with the lay of the land at WDW. Take Exit 64B off I-4, or if you are staying On Property, take WDW transportation to the park. If you are staying off Disney property, ask at the hotel desk for a shuttle to the park.

Here We Go If you drive your own car or a rental to the Studios, you will pay to park; you will park where told to by the Cast Members; and you will take the tram to the park entrance. Remember to remember where you put that vehicle. (Refer to this information in my section on the Magic Kingdom for more details.)

What Price Hollywood? That, of course, depends on the kind of ticket you want to buy. Tickets are available for purchase at the park entrance, where you can also present vouchers and acquire tickets, or present your Park Hopper tickets and go right in.

Hollywood or Bust You enter the Disney-MGM Studios on Hollywood Boulevard, which is actually much nicer here than the real one it is modeled after in the real city of Los Angeles. Enjoy the California architecture. Imagineers designed it to look as it might have looked in the Los Angeles area about 50 years ago (if it had been designed and maintained back then, by Disney.)

The hot tickets here are **The Twilight Zone Tower of Terror**, **Rock 'n' Roller Coaster Starring Aerosmith**, **Jim Henson's Muppet★Vision 3-D**, and the nightly show called **Fantasmic**.

Shopping There are more places to shop here than there are attractions, and for

©Disney 2003
Sci-Fi Dine-In Theater

movies buffs and television fans (that should include just about everyone), the shopping is excellent. The best of the bunch is **Sid Cahuenga's One-of-a-Kind**. This shop carries genuine movie memorabilia and signed movie star photos. It is pricey, but it is great for collectors and an interesting place for noncollectors to browse.

Dining The Table Service restaurants include *50's Prime Time Café*, *Hollywood Brown Derby*, *Mama Melrose's Ristorante Italiano*, and *Sci-Fi Dine-In Theater*. All these serve lunch and dinner. The *Brown Derby* is great when you feel like a more formal meal. My personal favorite is the *Sci-Fi Dine-In Theater*, set up like an old drive-in. It runs a 45-minute loop of loopy 1950s monster clips, trailers, and cartoons on a screen at the front of the restaurant.

Hollywood & Vine serves breakfast, lunch, and dinner, and this is where you can dine with the Disney characters. There are seven Quick Service restaurants and a number of food carts around the park for snacks. Finally, there are dinner packages at the Table Service restaurants that include reserved seating for the nighttime show, Fantasmic. Ask about those packages at the restaurants, at Guest Relations, or call **407-WDW-DINE (407-939-3463)**. Priority Seating is recommended for all the Table Service restaurants.

> **On with the Show** You can divide the attractions into two categories: those that run continuously and those that have specifically scheduled times. Knowing which is which should help you organize your day.

Attractions That Run Continuously

The Twilight Zone Tower of Terror You will find this thrill ride at the far end of Sunset Boulevard. Turn right onto Sunset off Hollywood Boulevard as you walk

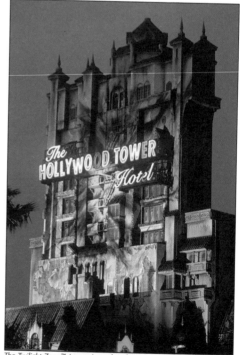

into the park. The pre-show here explains why this elevator is so out of control, as well as the Twilight Zone connection—doo dee Doo doo, doo dee Doo doo. The ride opened in 1994, and they keep reprogramming "the drop" to make it scarier, as if it weren't already heart-stopping enough. One glutton for punishment, a Central Florida woman over age 70, just received an honorary bellman's cap for riding this thing 500 times! In the post-show, you'll find pictures of yourself and your elevator mates snapped during the 13-story drop, and of course you can buy one of these, if you would like to do so. This ride is *very* popular, so consider FASTPASS. Minimum Height Requirement (MHR) is 40"/102 cm.

The Twilight Zone™ is a registered trademark of CBS, Inc. and is used pursuant to a license from CBS, Inc. ©Disney 2003

The Twilight Zone Tower of Terror

Also for the brave is **Rock 'n Roller Coaster® Starring Aerosmith**. The band recorded five soundtracks especially for this ride, and Stevie Tyler and Co. definitely deliver the decibels. Each Guest's seat has two high-frequency tweeters and

two mid-range speakers, with one subwoofer mounted under the seat, so you won't have any trouble hearing (or feeling) the tunes. (Your hearing *afterward* is another issue entirely.) There are 900 speakers in the entire attraction. Opened in 1999, this is The Studios' second thrill ride and the first at the Walt Disney World Resort that actually takes you upside down. You can't carry anything

©Disney 2003

Rock 'n Roller Coaster Starring Aerosmith

with you on the 1-minute 22-second experience, so park your stuff in a locker or give it to a friend before entering. This is at the end of Sunset Boulevard, right across from the Tower of Terror. Definitely not for those with fragile tweeters or subwoofers. FASTPASS. MHR 48"/122 cm.

Jim Henson's Muppet★Vision 3-D I'm a big fan of this attraction, which opened in 1991. It is on the other side of the park from the previous two attractions, so arrange your day with that in mind. It includes the wonderful mixture of sweet-and-sour humor common to all the Muppet features, as well as the exceptional attention to detail that is their hallmark. Take note of the signs and props around you as you queue up in the pre-pre-show. The actual pre-show is 12 minutes long and makes use of multiple television screens in a unique and funny way. The show, which is another 12 minutes, has the benefit of "critics" Statler and Waldorf sitting in the balcony, cracking wise, as usual, at the expense of the rest of the Muppets. Just as funny for adults as for kids, this is terrific entertainment. FASTPASS.

Star Tours Down at the same end of the park as the Muppets, this Star Wars attraction opened in 1990. You "ride" in a StarSpeeder, which is actually a simulator synchronized with a film, so the whole thing works a little bit like Body Wars at Epcot. The journey is 7 minutes long, and it can sometimes take an hour to get in, so use FASTPASS if you can. There is a lot of motion in this experience: expectant mothers are not allowed to ride. MHR 40"/102 cm.

The Great Movie Ride This 22-minute ride through movie history is inside the Chinese Theater at the center of the park. With clips and sound and Audio-Animatronic characters, it reviews some of the biggest stars and best-known dialogue in the movies. There are a couple of scenes that might scare meek children. It takes 25 minutes to reach the ride once you enter the building (assuming there is a full line ahead of you). No restrictions.

Disney-MGM Studios Backlot Tour You catch this tour on Mickey Avenue, and you reach that through the archway to the right as you face the Chinese Theater. Once through the arch, turn left. The tour begins at the end of the street. You start by watching a special effects show. Then, you board one of the trams for an actual tour of the Disney-MGM backlot. The post-show is a walk through the American Film Institute Showcase, which you can also visit without taking the tour. Plan on about 35-40 minutes for the entire thing.

©Disney 2003   *Catastrophe Canyon*

Also on Mickey Avenue you'll find the **Magic of Disney Animation**. It is a 35-minute experience that includes a movie and a meeting with a genuine Disney animator. These guys get the only covered parking at WDW, so you know they're special. Just down from this attraction is **Walt Disney: One Man's Dream**. Opened in 2001 for the 100 Years of Magic celebration, it was so popular with Guests that Disney decided to hold it over. The Walt Disney Company has an incredible archive in California, and for the first time, 400 items from this wonderful storehouse were pried from the grasp of Disney archivist Dave Smith. He's a great guy. He just hates to let the stuff out of his sight. The material was lovingly restored and flown to the Walt Disney World Resort on a special FedEx jet. The exhibits and film clips tell the story of Walt Disney, the remarkable founder of the entertainment empire. This is worth seeing, and you'd better do it while you can. You never know

©Disney 2003
Animators on the Disney-MGM Backlot Tour

when Dave Smith will want this stuff put back in the vault.

Honey, I Shrunk the Kids Movie Set Adventure is a creatively designed playground for kids. Little ones enjoy it, and you can use it to kill time while you wait for your FASTPASS reservation window for one of the E-Tickets.

Sounds Dangerous Starring Drew Carey is actually not dangerous at all, but lots of fun featuring this ABC star (Coincidence? I think not!). During the 12-minute show, Drew (who appears here electronically) tries to solve a crime, and while doing so, he wears a tiny camera in his tie, which, uh oh, he manages to lose. Hilarity—what else?—ensues. Some of this does take place in the dark, but it is generally not too intense for the little ones. You'll find this near Star Tours, to your left as you face the Chinese Theater.

"Plan Ahead" Attractions: Check Your Daily Times Guide for Schedules

Voyage of the Little Mermaid This 15-minute production debuted in 1992, and is a mixture of live performances, puppets, lasers, a lightning show, and film. It tells a condensed version of the movie, and it is one of the most popular attractions in the park. It's through the archway to the right as you face the Chinese Theater. FASTPASS.

The Indiana Jones Stunt Spectacular is a 35-minute show, down at the same end of the park as the Muppets. It opened in 1989, and though it has continued to entertain, it was relit and polished up a bit in 2003. It is a stunt show with a simple plot that involves Jones-ish adventures, villains, accidents, and fires, and it includes audience participation. Anyone want to play the villain? You will have the chance. There are 2,000 seats so you can usually get in, but FASTPASS is available if you need it.

Beauty and the Beast Live on Stage is performed in the Theater of the Stars off Sunset Boulevard. It is a Broadway-quality glimpse at this likable story. Belle is beautiful, the Beast has a heart of gold, and Lumière sings "Be Our Guest" with the place settings. If you can resist this, you probably have too much willpower.

TM & (©) 2003 The Jim Henson Company. JIM HENSON'S mark & logo, BEAR IN THE BIG BLUE HOUSE mark & logo, characters and elements are trademarks of The Jim Henson Company. All Rights Reserved. From the television series Bear in the Big Blue House created by Mitchell Kriegman. ©Disney 2003

Playhouse Disney–Live on Stage is especially good for small children. The 15-minute show features characters from the Disney Channel and is performed in the Animation Courtyard. There are no seats—everyone just sits on the floor, so be prepared.

Who Wants to Be a Millionaire–Play It The success of the ABC-TV program prompted this show, which opened as part of the "100 Years of Magic" celebration. Fast-fingered Guests are chosen to sit in the "hot seat," and though there are no million-dollar prizes, the rest of the rules are pretty much the same. Your "lifeline" is chosen at random from someone within the park that day (this is always a hoot), and as you leave you"ll be asking one another, "Is that your final answer?" FASTPASS.

To complete your visit, make plans to see **Fantasmic**, the best show in the park, one of the best at WDW. The laser-laden, fireworks-featuring spectacular is performed only in the evening. The amphitheater, just behind the Tower of Terror on Sunset Boulevard, holds nearly 7,000 people. Nevertheless, lines for the show can begin as early as 90 minutes ahead of showtime. Mickey appears as the Sorcerer's Apprentice and his dreams become a series of battles between the

©Disney 2003
*Honey, I Shrunk the Kids
Movie Set Adventure*

forces of good and the forces of evil. At the end of 26 minutes, you'll know who won. Some restaurants have packages that include reserved seating at Fantasmic. Call **407-939-3463** to make reservations.

©Disney 2003
*If you're interested in more formal dining,
the Hollywood Brown Derby Restaurant is excellent.*

©Disney 2003

Kilamanjaro Safaris®

THE ABSOLUTELY ESSENTIAL
ANIMAL KINGDOM

Entertainment WDW has added a layer of entertainment to this park that you won't see anywhere else On Property. Much of it is African in origin and takes place out-of-doors near Harambe Village, the little Kenyan-style town in AK's Africa. You may also see animal handlers who bring small creatures right onto the pathways to interact with Guests. There isn't a set schedule for these things, but they help make the park more interesting.

Parade During the AK's first few years of operation, many Guests chose to spend only half a day in the park. To discourage this, WDW instituted a parade in the afternoon designed to keep Guests from straying. The parades vary from year to year so visit the Web site at www.disneyworld.com for details and schedules.

Guests with Disabilities All the Disney parks are very accommodating to Guests with disabilities, and they continue to experiment with new ways to improve their service in this area. If this is a consideration for your family, ask at Guest Relations for the Guidebook for Guests with Disabilities. In some locations there are special Personal Translation Units for the visually impaired and for the hearing impaired. There are wheelchairs and personal electric vehicles (ECVs) for rent, and wheelchair access is standard in every Disney park. At the Animal Kingdom, many of the paths are a little rocky, in keeping with the wilderness theme, which means that of all the parks, the AK is the most challenging for Guests who are in wheelchairs or who have any difficulty walking. But as with all things Disney, Cast Members will go out of their ways to make sure your needs are met.

©Disney 2003

Disney's Animal Kingdom Lodge

Disney's Animal Kingdom Lodge   There are 30 hotels at the Walt Disney World Resort, and though all of them include the usual Disney quality, one is specifically worth a mention here. In April 2001, Disney's Animal Kingdom Lodge opened its doors. It overlooks the African savannah area of the Animal Kingdom, and that allows Guests to watch the animals in what appears to be a completely natural setting. I don't know of another hotel near a wild animal park in the United States that can boast of this feature. It is in the deluxe price category, but that doesn't mean you can't visit the Lodge for lunch, dinner, or a drink if you feel like looking around. Call **407-934-7639** for information on all the Disney hotels and resorts.

©Disney 2003

Conservation

DISNEY'S ANIMAL KINGDOM

The Animal Kingdom opened in 1998, and for a number of years before that, while the park was in development, the Walt Disney World Company made a full-time effort to consult the best of international conservationists on its plans. What emerged was a park dedicated to the theme of preservation, and that gives Disney's Animal Kingdom the strongest substance of any of its parks. There are 1,700 animals here, and the park opens early—often as early as 8:00 a.m.— so Guests can see the creatures when they are the most active. The Animal Kingdom will probably never have fireworks or a noisy nighttime show because this can disturb the animals. Clearly, even though Disney advertises this park as "Nah-tah-zu," it does have to be structured, to some extent, around the needs of the animals. At the same time Disney wants the park to be fun, so it has woven the stories of extinct creatures and creatures of the imagination into its theme.

The park's one serious issue is that the majority of its activities are outside. This makes sense for a park that features animals and animal conservation, but it can be a disadvantage during the Florida summer.

Hours The park opens early, because the animals are up and around with sunrise. It generally closes on or about dusk. Call **407-824-4321** or log on to www.disney-world.com for the opening and closing times during your visit.

On Safari All roads lead to the Animal Kingdom. Exit I-4 at 64B, and follow the signs to the park. From Kissimmee, take Osceola Parkway. On Property, take free buses to the front turnstiles, and off property catch available shuttles.

Parking The same drill as in the other parks. The early birds won't have to take the trams and will be able to walk to the entrance from the parking lot.

Sherpas Remember: this can be a hot park, and that is a very good reason not to bring heavy things to carry around. Your bags may need to be searched—another reason to travel light. For a fee, you can rent lockers here as in all the parks.

Not a Mirage As you enter, you are surrounded by a tropical oasis called, appropriately, the Oasis. It serves as both a pre-show when you enter and a post-show when you depart. There are animals here, but you have to look (up) for them. All the park traffic goes through here, and that can make this spot very crowded at opening and closing. Adjacent to the Oasis, is the only restaurant with Table Service at the Animal Kingdom. It is the *Rainforest Café*, where breakfast, lunch, and dinner are served. The eatery is what is known as a "themed restaurant," which means it serves up a sort of show with your meal. The meal portions are huge, so you might consider sharing a dish or two among your group. You can access this restaurant without entering the park, a feature that doesn't exist at any other WDW park restaurant. Priority Seating is recommended.

©Disney 2003
The Tree of Life

Hungry? Once past the Oasis and the *Rainforest Café*, you enter the park. While you have just left the only Table Service restaurant in your rearview mirror, there are 13 Quick Service places to eat ahead. Only one of them offers breakfast: *Restaurantosaurus* in DinoLand has a Character Breakfast that is entertaining, but is not inexpensive.

The Shape of Things
This park is shaped like a wheel with spokes. At its center is **Discovery Island**, which used to be called Safari Village. Whatever you call it, it is the central hub of the park. The Tree of Life is here and it serves as the park's symbol, as well as the home of the park's 3-D movie **It's Tough to Be a Bug!** The lines at "Bug" can

"It's Tough to be a Bug!" based upon the Disney/Pixar film "A Bug's Life" ©Disney/Pixar

be formidable: FASTPASS is available. From Discovery Island, the paths radiate outward to the park's four lands: **Africa; Asia; DinoLand U.S.A.;** and **Camp Minnie-Mickey**. Most of the animals are in **Africa** and **Asia**.

Africa

During the Millennium Celebration a Kikuyu artisan came from Nairobi, Kenya to make an appearance, and she spent a morning at the Animal Kingdom. When she returned to Epcot, she told me she was very surprised at how much like home Africa at the Animal Kingdom looked to her. The major attraction in AK's Africa is the **Kilimanjaro Safaris**, a trip in an open-air bus that gives you a chance to see the African animals in what looks like the wild. There are barriers between you and the animals, but they are designed to be difficult to spot, and this adds to the illusion that you really are on safari. The drive takes about 20 minutes and includes a story about ivory poachers. FASTPASS is available.

The Pangani Forest Exploration Trail is a self-guided walking tour that includes a number of stops in which you can see an aviary, an aquarium, a hippopotamus wallow ("Mud, mud, glorious mud … "), and an overlook of the savannah. It ends in a place where you can view silverback gorillas. The trail was originally called the Gorilla Falls Exploration Trail, but since there are no falls and you can't always see the gorillas, the name was changed. When you've walked back down the trail, you'll see the Harambe Train Station on your left. Here you can board the **Wildlife Express** for an experience called **Rafiki's Planet Watch** (formerly called

Conservation Station). This is an especially nice attraction for little children because it includes something called **Affection Section**, a Disney name for a petting zoo. At Rafiki's Planet Watch you will also see the behind-the-scenes care given to the park's 1700 resident animals, and hear an audio show on the sounds of the rain forest. The AK delivered a baby elephant in 2003, and you may get a chance to see it here before it is old enough to be released into the herd in the park. When you've had enough, just board the Wildlife Express back to Harambe Village, where there are places to eat, drink, and watch the terrific entertainment imported for this part of the park.

©Disney 2003
Kali River Rapids®

Asia

The E-Ticket in Asia is the attraction called the **Kali River Rapids**. When you visit Universal Studios Islands of Adventure, you'll see that their Bilge Rat Barges are

©Disney 2003
Maharaja Jungle Trek®

based on a similar system. Here, the back story concerns saving the rain forest from evil loggers and the setup is given during the pre-show at the "offices" of the Kali River Rapids Expedition Company. You then board a 12-person raft and hilarity ensues. (Have I said that before?) You will get very wet on this ride—though not quite as wet as you will on Universal's Bilge Rat Barges. In any case, be forewarned. It is helpful if you bring a beach towel or some dry clothing in your carry bag. MHR 38"/96.5 cm. Come first thing in the morning to avoid the lines or use FASTPASS. Family members who would rather sit this one out can take the **Maharaja Jungle Trek**, which is the Asia version of the Pangani Trail in Africa. It is a self-guided tour and includes the chance to spot some spectacular wildlife, including Asian tigers. Stop at the tin-roofed shack for a chance to get up close and personal with bats. Or not. Before you depart Asia, check the show times for **Flights of Wonder**, a 20-minute film featuring all kinds of winged creatures. From Asia, you will need to return to Discovery Island to take the route to either DinoLand U.S.A. or Camp Minnie-Mickey.

©Disney 2003

The Boneyard Dig Site

DinoLand U.S.A.

The thrill ride in **DinoLand** is Dinosaur (originally called Countdown to Extinction), a ride in a time machine (didn't I ride in a time machine back in Epcot?) to 65 million years BN (Before Now). Guests entering the "Dino Institute" are assigned the job of seeking out an iguanodon, and naturally enough, chaos ensues. I don't think this is *that* scary, but WDW warns it is too intense for many small children. MHR 40"/102 cm. Use FASTPASS if there is a line. The whole family will likely enjoy the show **Tarzan Rocks** in the Theater in the Wild, a live entertainment based loosely on the Edgar Rice Burroughs stories (but more closely related to the Disney animated film). The theater seats 1,500 people, and as a consequence it is very rare that those in the line don't make it in. Check your Times Guide & New Information sheet for show times. There are several other attractions here that small members of the family will like: the **Boneyard** is a playground designed to look like an archaeological dig. **Chester and Hester's Dino-Rama** is a new attraction (not unlike Mickey's Toontown Fair) just beyond the Boneyard, designed entirely for those junior members of your group.

Camp Minnie-Mickey

The final spoke that radiates from the Discovery Island hub takes you to this land dedicated to Disney characters. Each of the characters holds his "meet and greets" in a little safari shack here. Your Times Guide & New Information sheet will have the greeting schedule, and Cast Members in Camp Minnie-Mickey will also have all the details. Camp Minnie-Mickey features two live shows. **The Festival of the Lion King** is a 30-minute stage extravaganza that has so much going on, it is a little tough to take it all in: music, dancing, acrobatics, familiar songs from the film, and a fire juggler. Lots of people like to see this show, so check the performance schedule and come early. **Pocahontas and Her Forest Friends** has a conservation message featuring Grandmother Willow, Pocahontas, and well, some of Her Forest

Friends—real skunks, porcupines, and possums. For animal rights reasons there are very few performing animals in the AK. None in this group is rare, and they add to a very charming show.

Since this is the youngest of Disney's parks, it is still in the process of finding its way. New thrill rides are in the works, and there are plans to air-condition more of the attraction areas. In the meantime, its conservation message, which goes down with a spoonful of sugar, is an excellent one to share with your family.

©Disney 2003
Animals carved in The Tree of Life

MORE THINGS DISNEY

Hotels and Accommodations There are 30 hotels at the Walt Disney World Resort, with 33,000 rooms. Twenty of the hotels are owned by Disney. The other 10 are called "Official Hotels of Walt Disney World" and offer many of the same benefits without the storybook theming. Prices range from moderate to expensive. For information on all the rooms available at WDW, call **407-W-Disney (407-934-7639)** between 8:30 a.m. and 10:00 p.m. Eastern time. By the way, Disney is the only entertainment/travel company of its size (probably in the world) that still doesn't have an 800 number!

Nightlife Disney has expanded its out-of-the-park shopping and dining district in recent years. It now includes Pleasure Island (which requires a separate entrance fee); Marketplace, and a shopping district with the largest Disney store in the world, appropriately called World of Disney. Within the Marketplace, there is another Rainforest Café like the one at the Animal Kingdom. All of this adjoins Disney's West Side, which is similar in scope to Universal's CityWalk. It includes a 24-screen theater, restaurants, clubs, and entertainment. Self-parking is available all the way from Marketplace on one end to the West Side on the other. Take note: this complex is huge. Valet parking is available in the evenings.

Golf There are five 18-hole golf courses, and one family-play 9-hole course at WDW. The 18-hole courses include Osprey Ridge, Eagle Pines, Magnolia, Palm, and Lake

©Disney 2003

Fantasia Miniature Golf Course

Buena Vista. Oak Trail is the family-play 9-hole course. Call **407-WDW-PLAY (407-939-7529)** for tee times and other information.

Miniature Golf Fantasia Golf and Winter Summerland offer miniature golf. If you are staying On Property, hop the shuttle to the courses. Otherwise, take Exit 64 from I-4 onto resort property and just follow the signs.

Water, Water, Everywhere You can get as wet as you like at Blizzard Beach, Typhoon Lagoon, and River Country water parks, where swimming, slides, and wave pools abound. These have their own entrance fees. In addition, the Walt Disney World Resort has the largest rental fleet of watercraft in the world—more than 500 boats and personal watercraft are available for use on the Resort's waterways. Call **407-WDW-PLAY** for information.

©Disney 2003   *Downtown Disney's West Side*

Sports   Opened in 1997, the best feature of Disney's Wide World of Sports is its 7,500-seat baseball stadium. It is cozy and old-fashioned and has real grass on the field. In the spring you can catch the Atlanta Braves in training. The Harlem Globetrotters train at the field house. It sure is a shame there isn't full-time Major League Baseball at the WW of S.

Restaurants   There are almost too many choices here: WDW has 300 restaurants On Property. One of the best is ***California Grill*** at the top of the Contemporary Resort. If you schedule Priority Seating at the right time and are able to get a seat by the window, it is a great spot to watch the evening fireworks over at the Magic Kingdom. One feature offered by many of the restaurants is Disney's Junior Chef Program. Junior chefs get their own junior chef hats and jackets while real Disney chefs help them with things like decorating their own desserts or tossing the family's salad. The program is free: just ask about it at any Disney restaurant. Call **407-WDW-Dine (407-939-3463)** or go to www.disneyworld.com for dining information.

> **Weddings**   Disney has a Wedding Pavilion that handles more than 2,000 unions each year—isn't that an amazing number? If you are so inclined, the Disney wedding planners will even loan you Cinderella's glass carriage for the occasion—assuming you've found your Prince (or Princess) Charming. Call Disney's Fairy Tale Weddings at **407-828-3400**.

Guest Information   Cast Members are very well informed on all things Disney—from where to greet characters to how to get to the nearest miniature golf course—so feel free to ask them for help. Before you arrive, log on to www.disneyworld.com. Or call **407-824-4321**.

HOW UNIVERSAL STUDIOS TOURS BEGAN

Universal Studios began life as a real film studio. German immigrant Carl Laemmle started in the movie business the way a lot of the early moguls did: he owned a nickelodeon, which was an arcade sort of place that showed little movie loops for a nickel. These eventually evolved into silent movie theaters, and Laemmle began to realize that the business needed a steady stream of new films to keep it going. Laemmle also figured out that if he controlled production, he could make his business twice as profitable. In 1909, he founded the Independent Moving Picture Company, known as IMP, and by 1912, IMP had merged with five other production companies, to be renamed the Universal Film Manufacturing Company. In 1914, Laemmle decided to consolidate production on the West Coast, and to make that possible, he bought a 230-acre ranch in Los Angeles, which he dubbed Universal City.

A lot of the founding fathers of film were pretty tough characters. Carl Laemmle (pronounced LEM-lee) was known for being such a nice guy, his employees called him "Uncle Carl." (He also had a habit of employing numerous relatives—another source of the nickname.) He enjoyed showing people how movies were made, and once Universal City was up and running, he arranged to give tours to visitors and guests. From 1912 until Laemmle retired in 1936, the informal Universal Studios tour was part of the company's tradition.

After Laemmle retired, Universal went through several owners. By 1964, the company had merged with MCA. Originally a talent booking agency called the Music Corporation of America, MCA had become a global entertainment giant under the leadership of Lew Wasserman. MCA/Universal revived the studio tour. Most movies were being shot on location, and the tour (for which the company now charged a fee) was designed to make profitable use of all that Universal real estate. The tour began as a ride through Universal's Los Angeles back lot in a small tram, with stuntmen surprising visitors with shoot-outs and falls along the way. As the years went by, more sophisticated shows, rides, and attractions were added, and the tour began to stand on its own as a theme park.

THE ABSOLUTELY ESSENTIAL UNIVERSAL ORLANDO

Halloween Horror Nights Universal Studios in California was the home of all those classic monster movies of the 1930s, 1940s, and 1950s. Because of that, and because Universal does not have to live with the burden of the Disney

brand, it can be as gruesome as it wants to be in celebrating Halloween. That's why Universal's Halloween Horror Nights have become a big hit. You can pay to come in just for the evening events, or you can upgrade your ticket to include the nighttime activities. Either way, if Frankenstein and the Wolf Man and haunted houses give you a thrill, Universal is the place to be each October.

©2003 Universal Orlando. All Rights Reserved.

Mardi Gras Universal took note of the onslaught of college students coming to Florida during spring break and added this festival that continues to celebrate Mardi Gras long into Lent. It includes added live entertainment in the evenings at Universal Studios, Islands of Adventure, and CityWalk with lots of encouragement to party.

Schedules For the schedules on Halloween Horror Nights and Universal's Mardi Gras celebration, log on to www.universalorlando.com.

CityWalk This is the nighttime attraction at Universal, and it is located conveniently between Universal Studios and Islands of Adventure. Parking is free in the evening unless you want valet parking, which works very well here. For reservations, call **407-224-3663**. For information, call **407-363-8000** or log on to www.citywalkorlando.com.

Hotels The hotels at what Universal is calling the Universal Orlando Resort (sounds like the Walt Disney World Resort, hmm?) are a partnership between Universal and Loews, which runs the hotels. Guests at the hotels get automatic Universal Express access to all the rides. Call **407-503-7000** for reservations and information.

UNIVERSAL STUDIOS

Universal Studios opened in Orlando in 1990. The park was built on land that had long been an orange grove, and back then, it seemed to be a nice, quiet attraction situated in the middle of—forgive me, Orange County—the boondocks.

In the decade since then, Universal Studios has grown with amazing speed. The first park now has about five or six times the number of attractions it had on opening day. A second park—Universal's Islands of Adventure—is up and running, and the complex includes three hotels, an enormous parking garage, and a nighttime entertainment zone called CityWalk.

> Universal has done a wonderful job with this destination. The landscaping includes tall palm trees, and low sea grass evocative of the first Universal Studios in California, and the parks offer almost exactly the same amenities as those offered by the Walt Disney World Resort. Imitation, after all, is the sincerest form of competition.

Universal has some features visitors will like. There is one central place to park, and all the foot traffic is funneled from the parking garage directly to CityWalk and the two parks. This means that once you have left your vehicle in the parking garage or arrived by shuttle, you need not take any other journeys by car or bus to enjoy Universal. From CityWalk, one pathway leads to the gates of Universal Studios and another leads to the gates of Islands of Adventure. The central garage provides covered parking, another real bonus in Florida. Without Disney's vast acreage, Universal has made a virtue of its more compact logistics.

The biggest challenge faced by Universal Studios as a destination, is that its ownership has changed so many times since the park opened in 1990. Just a year after the opening, MCA/Universal was bought by Matsushita Electrical Industrial Company of Japan. In 1995, the Seagram Company Ltd. bought the majority interest in Universal from Matsushita. In June 2000, Seagram combined with Vivendi and Canal of France—the owner of a string of luxury brands—to create Vivendi Universal. In the summer of 2003, Universal was "in play" (as the investment bankers put it) yet again. Employees must have to check the business section of the newspaper periodically to figure out whom they are working for. Somehow, in spite of all these changes at the top, Universal Studios, has continued to improve the quality of its product. How they've managed it, I don't know, but it is a lucky thing for vacationers that they have.

En Route   Universal is just 12 miles from the Orlando city limits. But it is more than 20 miles from Kissimmee so its convenience depends on your location. The three hotels at Universal—Portofino Bay, the Hard Rock Hotel, and the Royal Pacific Hotel—have water taxis and shuttles to the parks. If you are driving, take Exit 74B off I-4. Many hotels have

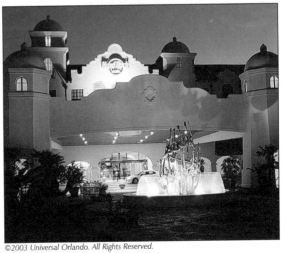

The Hard Rock Hotel

their own shuttles to Universal, and if your hotel does not, ask for a Universal shuttle to come pick you up. In addition, easy directions from all over Central Florida are available at www.universalorlando.com.

Parking There is a parking fee at Universal, just as there is at Disney, but as I mentioned earlier, there is one advantage here not available at the Walt Disney World Resort: covered parking. This means that when you return to your vehicle, it will not be a billion degrees inside, which is a very nice thing. Write down or remember the name and row number of your parking spot. During some times of the year, Universal offers "priority parking," which, I gather, is a little closer to the park. Being thrifty, I didn't spring for it. At night, there is valet parking for CityWalk, and it is exceptionally well managed. I highly recommend using it.

Please Stand to the Left Moving sidewalks are available to take you from the parking garage to CityWalk and the park entrances. This is another terrific feature. There is always plenty of walking involved in a theme park visit; the moving sidewalks make the beginning and end of the day much more pleasant. (I sure wish they had something like this within the parks themselves.)

There are 13 restaurants and clubs in Universal's CityWalk.

CityWalk This is the first part of the complex you see when you have finished your journey from the parking garage. It is a big, long, sweep of restaurants, bars, clubs, and eateries, all of which begin to rock in the evening. Some of the clubs have cover charges, and deals are available that combine a fixed-price dinner with entrance to some of the clubs. Visit www.universalorlando.com for more information on the deals available at CityWalk.

Are We There Yet? If you are going to Universal Studios, turn right at the CityWalk carousel and continue on over the bridge. You will see the gates of the park ahead of you. They are copies of the original gates of the first Universal Studios in California, through which passed movie stars such as Lon Chaney, Rudolph Valentino, Tony Curtis, Boris Karloff, Donald O'Connor, and Doris Day. Machines that dispense tickets are to the right as you walk toward the gates. The ticket windows are directly ahead of you. If you plan to visit more than one of the parks, consider one of their 2-day, 2-park tickets. These let you move from park to park with ease, and since everything is fairly close together here, these tickets allow your family to split up and meet back at CityWalk later in the day, if that is what you would like to do.

If you can't find something fun to do at Universal's CityWalk, you aren't paying attention.

Check it Out At 110 acres, Universal Studios is almost exactly the same size as the Magic Kingdom at the Walt Disney World Resort. Where the Magic Kingdom is a circle, Universal is more of an oval that sits on a diagonal, between 1 o'clock and 7 o'clock, with a lagoon at its center. This is a very easy park to navigate. Its size is comfortable to negotiate in a day, and almost all the attractions are inside, where visitors can enjoy the blessings of air conditioning. It is a good-looking park with good queueing plans and a well-trained staff. Universal has watched Disney closely and stolen from that company's experience which, in business, is not against the law.

Through the Gates The **Front Lot** is the area closest to the park's entrance. This is where you will find Guest Services, ATMs, restrooms, pay phones, guides for those with disabilities, etc. You can rent wheelchairs here, as well as lockers, and the lockers are handy if you brought sunhats or rain jackets you don't want to carry around all day. Snacks are available at the **Fudge Shoppe** and the **Beverly Hills Boulangerie**, the latter of which has umbrella-shaded tables on the sidewalk, where it is nice to sit and go over the Studio Guide Map and Attraction & Show Times guide to plan your day. The map and the guide are available at the front gate and at Guest Services stations throughout the park.

Production Central Things are changing at Production Central. Out are **Hitchcock's 3-D Theater** and the **Funtastic World of Hanna-Barbera**. Both of these attractions have been very popular, but they are being replaced by experiences that will speak to a younger generation: **Jimmy Neutron's Nicktoon Blast™** and **Shrek 4-D™**. **Nickelodeon Studios® Gamelab** is open on a schedule available in your Attractions & Show Times guide. There is a chance you can be in the audience when they are taping shows at Nickelodeon Studios—usually in the afternoon and not every day. Ask for tickets in front of Nickelodeon, near the **Green Slime™ Geyser**. **SoundStage 54** has vehicles from Universal movies—the cars from the *Mummy Returns* and *Blue Crush*, for example. **Monsters Café** is a fast-food joint with Frankenstein and Dracula décor; if you arrive early, you'll want to move on and visit most of these places later.

Jimmy Neutron's Nicktoon Blast™

New York Continue straight on Plaza of the Stars and you'll gradually see the buildings make a transition from a back lot look to the look of New York City. The street becomes 57th Street, and on the left you will come to **Twister … Ride It Out®**. This is one of the park's hot tickets, but there is no "riding" involved here. After a pre-show, you are led into a large soundstage (no seats), where there is a special-effects show representing what a twister might do to a small town. The special effects are pretty good, but I could see the strings on the flying cow (uh oh, I gave it away) and I think you are standing too close to seriously suspend your disbelief. I talked to some people who really enjoyed it, though, so perhaps I was not in the proper frame of mind. Universal has a new line-busting system similar to FAST-PASS, called Universal Express™, and it is available for Twister. Also in New York, **Extreme Ghostbusters**, the **Blues Brothers**,

Twister ... Ride It Out®

and **Street Breaks** are shows presented on a daily schedule: you should consult your Attraction & Show Times guide for more details. Eateries in New York are *Finnegan's Bar & Grill*, for full service meals, and *Louie's Italian Restaurant*.

San Francisco As you leave New York, South Street turns into the Embarcadero and everything around you begins to look like the City by the Bay. What better place to experience **Earthquake®—The Big One** than in this city nestled against the San Andreas Fault? The first part of this attraction is a pre-show that unlocks some of the secrets of special effects in the movies and includes audience participation. The second part is a ride in a Bay Area Rapid Transit (called BART in SF) vehicle that just happens to be rolling when "the Big One" hits. Both parts are excellent, and if the lines are long, use Universal Express. The other show (also with Express) in SF is **Beetlejuice's Graveyard Revue™**. It is listed as a "PG-13" show, but most members of your family will find it to be good, clean monster fun. If you are hungry, *Lombard's Seafood Grille* has a great location right on the lagoon; the *San Francisco Pastry Co.* has fast food, snacks, and of course, latte, this being the Left Coast. (I'm a Bay Area native so I can say this with impunity.)

Amity This is one of the best-looking sets in the park. It has a big shark icon in its center, which is a very popular place to have a picture taken with one's head in the shark's mouth (I saw quite a few young boys delighted to do this). The ride **Jaws®**, in Amity, is at least as goofy and fun as the Jungle Cruise at Disney, and at one point there is a fire that I'm pretty sure singed my eyebrows. Universal Express is available. Amity is about halfway around the park, and many people stop here to replenish the system. At **Richter's Burger Co.**, you can create your own burger. **Captain Quint's Seafood and Chowder Restaurant** provides the obvious, and fast food and snacks can be found at **Boardwalk Funnel Cake Co.**, **Brody's Ice Cream Shoppe**, and the **Midway Grill**. The entire area looks like one of those nice seaside boardwalks we used to have in America before a lot of them got kind of sleazy.

World Expo Boy, does this part of the park look like Future World at Epcot! It contains two very popular rides. The first you'll come to as you leave Amity is **Men in Black™ Alien Attack™**. I found that since I was there solo, I could enter through the singles line and save a lot of time. (If you can't do this, you can use Universal Express.) I figured this was a ride designed just for teenagers, but I was wrong, wrong, wrong. It

is tons o' fun—the best ride in the park. Because of the interactive piece—you get to shoot aliens as you ride—it is the kind of ride you will want to go on again and again (gotta see if you can improve that score!) The other attraction in World Expo is **Back to the Future The Ride®**. It includes an overlong pre-show and then moves into the ride part, which is a simulator-style attraction. The simulator rocks

©2003 Universal Orlando. All Rights Reserved.
Men In Black™ Alien Attack™

and lunges a lot, and even if you don't tend to motion sickness, it might bother you that your head keeps getting slammed against the back of the seat. Whiplash is fun? I did get a laugh from the pre-show scene with the test dummies. Universal designers were having some fun sending up Test Track over at Epcot. As you leave **Back to the Future**, there is a place where you can get a soft drink and stand inside a bottle-sort-of-thing and cool down. World Expo also has the **International Food and Film Festival** which is a food court showing old Universal film clips.

Woody Woodpecker's KidZone This is the park-within-a-park for the little guys. All the attractions here are playgrounds or shows that run on a schedule except the **E.T. Adventure®**, a ride designed by Steven Spielberg with a little story about helping E.T. go home. Each passenger is issued a "passport", and you'll understand the reason when you take the ride. Taking the name of each rider and issuing each a passport takes time and causes the lines to grow long on even the quietest day, and I'm not sure the pay-off is worth it. Use Universal Express for this one. The other KidZone attractions are **Animal Planet Live!™** (a little bit like Pets Ahoy at

SeaWorld, Universal Express is available), **A Day In the Park with Barney™** (25 minutes, little kids love it, and Universal Express is available), **Curious George Goes to Town** (an interactive playground), **Woody Woodpecker's Nuthouse Coaster®** (you have to be 36"/91.4 cm tall to ride), and **Fievel's Playland®**. The KidZone characters appear and sign autographs here. To keep sticky hands from goo-ing up the attractions, food is for sale only on the fringes of KidZone.

Hollywood   As you loop back toward the front gates, you re-enter Hollywood, another really excellent Universal "set." In this last section of the park you will find one of the most popular attractions in the entire place: **Terminator 2: 3-D Battle Across Time™**. It includes live actors, some "armed" robots, and a 3-D film that stars Arnold Schwarzenegger. With the pre-show, the entire experience takes about 25 minutes and is definitely one of the park's best productions. Universal Express is available, and the attraction is so popular you would be advised to use it.   Universal labels this a PG-13 show, and by that I think they mean that it is really too frightening for tiny children. After **T2 3D** everything else is anti-climax. The **Universal Horror Make-Up Show** is presented on a schedule, and **Lucy A Tribute** is a walk-through for Lucy fans. Hollywood has lots of nice places to eat: *Café La Bamba* is well situated with tables in a California-like patio; *Mel's Drive-In* has burgers and other fast food; *Schwab's Pharmacy* is set up like an old-fashioned drugstore with a counter; and the *Beverly Hills Boulangerie* is where we came in, isn't it?

Terminator 2: 3-D Battle Across Time™

UNIVERSAL'S
ISLANDS OF ADVENTURE

Almost nine years after Universal opened its first park, the company produced its second park, Islands of Adventure, next door. It is the same size as Universal Studios Florida—110 acres—but it is an entirely different kind of place. The music is louder, the sets are more over-the-top, the rides are edgier, and the target audience is younger. Not that the valiant and the spry over the age of 30 won't enjoy it, and not that there isn't lots for the tots—I'm just trying to outline the general feeling of the place.

If the weather is hot, you might want to wear a swimsuit under a cover-up to this park. If the weather is cool, you should bring along a change of clothing. Several of the rides get you good and drenched at Islands of Adventure, and unless you like the adventure of walking around in wet clothing, you need to be prepared for this. The rides that get you wet are fun—and you don't want to miss them just because you fear being wet for the rest of the day. Wearing something like nylon running gear that dries quickly is another alternative.

Moving Right Along If you are driving, take Exit 74-B off I-4, just as you would for Universal Studios Florida. Shuttle service is available from most local hotels, and all the Universal hotels have transportation to the parks. For Universal hotel information and directions to the park from all over Florida, log on to www.universalorlando.com.

> **Park and Ride** The one central garage is an advantage at Universal. As I mentioned in the previous section, the parking is covered, which keeps your vehicle from heating up to a rapid boil while you are in the parks, and the central location of the garage is very handy. You need to park your vehicle only once to enjoy Islands of Adventure, CityWalk, and Universal Studios. They threw in those moving sidewalks to make it easier to get from the garage to the attractions, and oh how nice they are.

CityWalk to Islands When you hop off the moving sidewalks you arrive at CityWalk. If you arrive early in the morning as your Absolutely Essential guide writer continually suggests you do, you will find most of CityWalk quiet, preparing to get nutty later in the day. In the morning, CityWalk serves as a boardwalk you traverse to get to the park. Pass the first sign for Universal Studios, and take the second turn to your right, just past Margaritaville, to Islands of Adventure.

Open Sesame The gates of Islands look like something out of an old *Sinbad* movie—which I think is exactly what they are designed to represent. The adjacent icon is called the Pharos Lighthouse and I'm not quite sure what it does, but at 130 feet tall it is definitely un-miss-able. Ticket windows are straight ahead. All the usual services for visitors are in a semicircle to your right and to your left.

Port of Entry This preshow is very impressive looking but there isn't much you will want to do here early in the day. Later, you might want to come back to eat, shop, and enjoy the Middle-Eastern-bazaar-like atmosphere but if you've come here for the hot tickets, it's best to move right along. When I came here on a recent

Mardi Gras in the spring is a big event at Islands of Adventure

visit (through the gates at the 9:00 a.m. opening, just as you should do, dear reader), everyone I saw who reached the lagoon at the end of Port of Entry turned left and headed over to Marvel Super Hero Island. Being the contrarian that I am, this was my signal to turn right, and I was richly rewarded in my counterclockwise travel with no wait times at any of the rides *until* I arrived at Marvel Super Hero Island, my last stop. That is how I'm going to direct you here, but once again all route suggestions are optional. Pick up an Adventure Guide (park map) and Attraction & Show Times guide at the entrance to help you make your decisions. You can also get park maps before you arrive by logging on to www.universalorlando.com.

> **Park Layout** Islands of Adventure is laid out around a central lagoon, and if you turned to the right from Port of Entry upon reaching the lagoon and moved counterclockwise, you would find the "islands" in this order: **Seuss Landing**, the **Lost Continent**, **Jurassic Park**, **Toon Lagoon**, and **Marvel Super Hero Island**.

Seuss Landing I went straight to the **Cat in the Hat™** ride here, since as a six year old I tortured my parents by memorizing this book and reciting it to them over and over and over. If you've read the book with your children, which I hope you have (warning: don't let any of them memorize it), all of you will enjoy this little ride

©2003 Universal Orlando. All Rights Reserved.
Oh, Dr. Seuss, what have you wrought?

through the story. The cars spin delightfully and Thing One and Thing Two enjoy featured roles as the twin troublemakers. The rest of Seuss Landing is strictly for tots, which is a good thing, since the other "islands" may be a bit much for them. There is a carousel— called **Caro-Seuss-el™**; a little aerial ride called **One Fish, Two Fish, Red Fish, Blue Fish™**; and a playground called **If I Ran the Zoo™**. There are four places to shop, including a really nice, all-Seuss bookstore called **All the Books You Can Read**. There are four places to eat, and all have great small-fry food, including the classic PBJ (peanut butter and jelly sandwich). The ***Green Eggs and Ham Café*** has—but of course—a Green Eggs and Ham Sandwich.

The Lost Continent Two thrill rides are the main features of this island. Called **Dueling Dragons®**, they are a pair of roller coasters that do the absolute maximum that roller coasters can do to scare you into a sanitarium. People seem to love them. The pre-show is a quarter-mile walk through a tunnel, where guests are told the story behind these two elements of torture, I mean, rides. One dragon coaster is called **Fire** and one is called **Ice** and if you feel like doing this to yourselves, have at it. I tried the smaller **Flying Unicorn**® (I know, I'm a chicken), which they tell me is a coaster aimed at ages 6 through 12. It was

still way too scary for me, though on the positive side, it was mercifully short. The two other attractions in the Lost Continent are shows: the **Eighth Voyage of Sinbad**®, a special-effects-stunt show, (closed during some special events) and **Poseidon's Fury**®, a walk-through show, during which Zeus takes on Poseidon and thunderbolts and crashing waves abound. There is

Dueling Dragons

a fortune teller's tent in this land and four places to get snacks and quick meals. The **Mythos Restaurant** provides a full table service menu for lunch and dinner, and though it is not inexpensive, it is a serene spot in which to get away from the hurly burly. The food—from Wood Oven Pizza to Cedar Planked Salmon—is first rate.

Jurassic Park The best thing here is the **Jurassic Park River Adventure**®, a sort of cross between Jaws (the ride) and Disney's Splash Mountain. The adventure begins quietly enough; but, when the not-so-peaceful dinosaurs appear, you're "for it" as the Brits would say. If you are tall enough (42"/106 cm), plan to get your hair good

and wet and also expect to laugh. The **Triceratops Discovery Trail** is a walk-through close encounter that young children will especially enjoy. The **Jurassic Park Discovery Center**® is an interactive center and a nice place to pause, as it is indoors and air-conditioned. **Camp Jurassic**® is a themed playground, which also features the **Pteranodon Flyers**®, a Dumbo-like ride for kids with a Jurassic theme.

Toon Lagoon If you are still damp from the Jurassic Park River Adventure, you might as well head straight for **Dudley Do-Right's Ripsaw Falls**® in Toon Lagoon. The pre-show/queuing

The Jurassic Park River Adventure

area seems incredibly long, even when there is no wait time, and I especially didn't like seeing the rusted metal trough above me leaking water on my head. However, when I finally got onto the ride, I just hung on for dear life—and laughed—with the rest of the crowd. You ride through the water in a vehicle shaped like a log, and when you reach the top of the falls, you drop 60 feet into even more water, which splashes everywhere, especially on the people at the very front of the vehicle, er, log. Unless you are a total grouch, this should crack you up. If your hair was wet in Jurassic Park, quite a lot more of you will be wet now. But there is more water to come!

On a recent visit, I wrung myself out as best I could, and headed over to **Popeye & Bluto's Bilge-Rat Barges**®. As I was waiting to get on, I noticed people getting off the ride wearing swimsuits. How wet could this be, I wondered? Very wet, as it turns out. The ride is designed to make you look as if you stood in the shower with all your clothes on. Great fun especially on a hot day—but, as I pointed out earlier, you should definitely bring a change of clothes if you want to enjoy the rest of your visit. What I didn't realize until later was that people using the adjacent playground, called **Me Ship, The Olive**, can use water cannons to shoot at the barges, which causes barge riders to get even wetter, much to the merriment of the parkgoers over at the Olive. Ha Ha. While I sat and attempted to dry off, I had a very good half chocolate/half vanilla soft ice cream in a waffle cone from *Cathy's Ice Cream*. Comfort food is always a nice idea.

Just ahead, **Comic Strip Lane** looks like the Sunday funnies writ large, and there are lots of places to eat and shop as you head over to **Marvel Super Hero Island**. Before you depart, check your Attraction & Show Times guide for the schedule on **Mat Hoffman's Crazy Freakin' Stunt Show!!!**—it is hot stuff for the skateboarding X-treme crowd.

The Incredible Hulk Coaster is so incredible, I suggest you ride it in my place.

Marvel Super Hero Island This is a land designed for teens, college students, and other fearless thrill seekers. While they party here, Mom and Dad might want to go back to Port of Entry for a nice, quiet hour at one of the cafés. In the meantime, the braver sorts of all generations will line up for **Doctor Doom's Fearfall**®. It features the same kind of equipment used in Disney's Tower of Terror, but it creates a somewhat more frightening experience because you drop completely out in the open. I tried one of these things at a theme park convention several years ago, so I wasn't inclined to do this to myself again. The ride takes you up 150 feet, and the subsequent drop is actually a controlled one, but it surely doesn't feel like it. You have to be 52"/132 cm

©2003 Universal Orlando. All Rights Reserved.
The Amazing Adventures of Spiderman

to ride, and the lines get long late in the day. Family members who crave this sort of excitement should consider coming here first thing in the morning. Ditto for the **Incredible Hulk Coaster®**. Definitely take everything out of your pockets and off your head (glasses and hats will fall off and get lost) and place all this in the lockers available at the front of the ride. The Hulk takes you upside down I-don't-know-how-many times, and even though I just saw a program on the Discovery Channel about how safe these things are, I still don't like going upside down. However, if you're not inclined to ride, it's still fun to stand and watch the people on the coaster as they become inverted. The height requirement for Hulk is 54"/137 cm.

Those not tall enough to partake can walk over to **Storm Force Accelatron®**, a themed ride with no height restrictions, designed for younger park goers (check your Attraction & Show Times guide for details). The final hot ticket here is the **Amazing Adventures of Spiderman®**. It uses a creative mix of 3-D and thrill ride and is so popular, there is always a wait time. The minimum height requirement for Spiderman is 40"/102 cm. All the attractions in Marvel Super Hero Island have Universal Express, an indication of how popular this section of the park is.

One final observation: I took you counterclockwise around Islands, and it meant few lines as I headed in that direction, from Seuss Landing through Jurassic Park. However, thrill seekers should do the opposite; turn left at the end of Port of Entry and head straight for Marvel Super Hero Island and Toon Lagoon at the beginning of the day. Those two areas have the most popular attractions in the park and since there is rarely a quiet time in either Hero or Toon, heading there early makes the most sense.

An Introduction to SeaWorld
SEA-ING THE WORLD

Theme parks are such big business these days, it is difficult to imagine a time when a few guys just sat down, thought one up, built it, and watched the money roll in. But that is just how Sea World began. Four fraternity brothers from the University of California at Los Angeles got together in 1962 and had the idea to build a restaurant in San Diego with some kind of marine animal show. The more they talked about it, the more the idea expanded until Milton Shedd, George Millay, Ken Norris, and Dave DeMott were building the world's first theme park featuring marine animals. Sea World opened in San Diego in 1964, and the rest, as they say, is history. Along the way, Sea World acquired its first orca, or killer whale, and named it Shamu. Shamu® is now a registered trademark.

The publishing house Harcourt Brace Jovanovich bought the parks in 1976 and ran them until 1989, when HBJ sold Sea World to Busch Entertainment Corporation, one of 13 companies under the umbrella of Anheuser-Busch, Inc.

©2003 SeaWorld of Florida

The new owners did make some changes. The park added its first thrill ride, **Journey to Atlantis**, in 1998, installed its second, **Kraken**, in 2000, and launched a nighttime entertainment complex, **WaterFront at SeaWorld**, in 2003.

All this upgrading has been accomplished without taking anything away from the features that make SeaWorld (that's the new Busch spelling) unique—its marine mammal shows and other animal attractions. Not as slick as Disney, not as teen-oriented as Universal, SeaWorld has an appeal to anyone with an appreciation for and a love of nature. The park still does not sell drinks with plastic lids or disposable plastic straws, or launch helium-filled balloons during its shows in order to protect the safety of creatures within the park and beyond.

THE ABSOLUTELY ESSENTIAL SEAWORLD

SeaWorld Adventure Camp SeaWorld is set up to handle school groups of all kinds. The SeaWorld Education Department offers more than 200 different summer camp adventures, including sleepover programs for students as well as for the whole family. One program specifically targets teens interested in careers in the biological sciences. For information, call **407-363-2380**.

Budweiser Beer School The Anheuser-Busch Hospitality Center in the park is home to this program that shows visitors how Busch "uses the finest ingredients to brew Budweiser, the top-selling beer in the world!" In the course of the school, you'll get to taste several varieties of the product. These are small tastes, and sampling is limited to guests 21 years of age and older. Check the back of your park map for the BBS schedule.

Orlando Flex Ticket SeaWorld, Universal Studios Florida, Universal Studios Islands of Adventure, and the water park Wet 'n Wild have teamed up to offer a 4-park multiday ticket designed to compete with the Park Hopper ticket at the Walt Disney World Resort. A 5-park multiday ticket is also available that includes the parks above as well as Busch Gardens Tampa Bay. For information and reservations call **800-224-3838**. Shuttle information is available at **800-221-1339**. Log on to www.seaworld.com and you'll find multiday ticket information as well.

Meetings and Conventions SeaWorld is a great venue for a party, and the park in fact hosts more than 400 such events every year. Call **407-363-2200** for information on booking.

WaterFront This is SeaWorld's new nighttime venue designed to compete, one would imagine, with Downtown Disney and CityWalk at Universal. SeaWorld's WaterFront is somewhat different in that it requires an entrance ticket to the park, which the other nighttime venues do not. A nighttime venue

©2003 SeaWorld of Florida
The WaterFront at SeaWorld

inside a theme park would seem to have a very different appeal from one that exists outside a theme park. You be the judge.

©2003 SeaWorld of Florida

*If you saw nothing else but the Shamu Adventure,
your visit to SeaWorld would be worthwhile.*

SEAWORLD ADVENTURE PARK

eaWorld is a wonderful park that has retained its old-Florida feel as it has modernized and moved into the 21st century. On a recent visit, I noticed lots of school children visiting in groups, wearing matching T-shirts, and taking guided tours of the park. I don't want to use the "e" word—education—too often here, because it might be a turn-off to some, but this is a park where you can both learn and play. If many of the experiences at this park don't cause you to marvel at the wonders of the world around you, you may be visiting the wrong park for your personality.

Park Ahoy! If you are headed east (toward Daytona Beach from points south of downtown Orlando), you reach SeaWorld Adventure Park by taking Exit 71 off I-4. This will take you onto the Central Florida Parkway, and from there you just follow the signs. If you are headed west on I-4 (toward Tampa from downtown Orlando), take Exit 72. This will put you briefly onto the Bee Line Expressway. Take the first exit off the Bee Line and follow the signs. SeaWorld has very easy access from the interstate, so once you take the exits I've just mentioned, you are only a few minutes from the parking lot.

Park 'n' Walk There is no covered parking here, but if you come early, you will be able to park very close to the entrance and you will have an easy walk to the front turnstiles. Remember all the usual admonitions about parking: don't leave anything in the car that could be damaged by heat (pets come to mind along with lipstick and lunch); always lock the car; and remember where you've parked. There is a parking fee.

> **You Open Yet?** SeaWorld is open from 9:00 a.m. year-round with extended hours during summer and holidays. This means at non peak times the park will close at 7:00 p.m., and at other times, will remain open until 10:00 p.m. For park hours during your visit and general park information, call **407-351-3600**.

Open, Sez Me I don't want to set the Justice Department's cartel squad on these theme park people, but it seems very interesting that the Walt Disney World Resort, Universal Studios, and SeaWorld Adventure Park all seem to charge almost exactly the same ticket prices. Coincidence? Hmm? Feel free to ask for discounts on your tickets. Recently a friend requested and received a senior discount at SeaWorld. Tickets are available at the ticket windows at the front of the park. For information on buying tickets in advance call **407-351-3600** or log on to www.seaworld.com.

Eateries At SeaWorld Adventure Park you'll find 12 places to dine and get refreshments, and four special event dining opportunities. To compare: at the Magic Kingdom at WDW, which is about the same size as SeaWorld, there are 24 places to eat. The numbers speak for themselves, and this reduced refreshment opportunity is worth remembering as you plan your day. Three of the four special event dining opportunities require reservations (they call a reservation a reservation at SeaWorld), and all might be of interest to you and your family. **Dine with Shamu** is a poolside buffet adjacent to Shamu Stadium that allows you to see the orcas up close and talk with their trainers. **Sharks Underwater Grill** is a full-service restaurant in a man-made grotto that is reminiscent of the Coral Reef at Epcot's Living Seas. Finally, the **Makahihi Luau** (formerly called the Aloha Polynesian Luau Dinner and Show) is held each evening at the

©2003 SeaWorld of Florida
Dining at SeaWorld is fun and informal.

Seafire Inn. Call **407-351-3600** to schedule these dining experiences or stop by the Information Counter at the front of the park.

During the day, at the *Seafire Inn* your meal becomes part of *Rico & Roza's Musical Feast.* This does not require reservations, but you are urged to come at least 15 minutes before show time. Show times are listed on the back of your park map. *Voyager's Wood Fired Pizza* is the newest full-service restaurant in the park. Fast food and more casual dining are offered at the *Cypress Bakery*, the *Polar Parlor*, the *SandBar*, *Hospitality Deli*, *Mango Joe's Café*, *Mama Stella's Italian Kitchen*, *Captain Pete's Island Eats*, and the *Smoky Creek Grill*. New places for quick eats at the WaterFront include *Freeza's*, *Café De Mar*, and *Smugglers Feasts*.

Information, Please! To your left as you enter the park you'll see the park's Information Counter. (There are several counters actually, but they all serve a guest services function and labor under the one name.) If you want to make arrangements for special tours, this is where you will do that. You can also make dining reservations here, as mentioned earlier, and may request any special assistance you will need.

SeaWorld has added a number of special programs to its park menu, and these can be booked at the Information Counter, or booked in advance by calling **800-432-1178**. They are all limited in size and offer guests terrific opportunities and

©2003 SeaWorld of Florida

The Whale Swim Adventure

experiences, but all of them have an added cost, and some of the costs are quite high. (In 2003 the prices ranged from an added $125 per person up to an added $389 per person, though some include a park entrance or a 7-day park pass in that fee.) **Sharks Deep Dive** allows you to snorkel or scuba dive in a shark cage. The **Whale Swim Adventure** is a 2-hour program allowing you to interact with a

with false killer whales. The only program of its kind in North America, it is limited to just four guests at a time. The **Marine Mammal Keeper Experience** is a daylong tour that begins at 6:30 a.m. and includes a chance to work along with the park's marine mammal experts. **Trainer for a Day** allows guests to shadow SeaWorld animals trainers. The **Adventure Express Tour** gives guests a 7-hour guided VIP tour with no waiting in line for any of the attractions. Since SeaWorld doesn't have a FASTPASS® system, this is your only opportunity to "back door the attractions" as they say in the theme park business. **To the Rescue, Polar Expedition Tour**, and **Predators** are all much-lower-cost adventures ($10 per person in 2003) that take guests backstage for short visits in specific areas with SeaWorld experts. For advance information on any of these, call **800-432-1178**.

Plan Ahead There is much more to do here than you could ever manage in a day, so don't get discouraged if you can't do it all before you collapse into a heap. This is such a pretty park, you won't mind coming back. In this park there is no real advantage to turning right after you enter, and taking a contrarian path counterclockwise to avoid the crowds. The only feasible route is the one everyone will take, and that is clockwise around what is essentially the wide oval of SeaWorld. As is true of Disney-MGM Studios, SeaWorld's attractions can be divided into rides and experiences that run continuously,

©2003 SeaWorld of Florida

Journey to Atlantis

and shows that run on a schedule. If you would like to pack as much as possible into the available hours, you may want to get a park map at the entrance, review it carefully, and plan your day.

My advice is to come early (at opening) and do two loops of the park. Most of the shows don't begin until 11:00 a.m. If you enter at 9:00 a.m., you will have 90 minutes to do one quick loop, heading for the rides and attractions that may be crowded later in the day, such as **Journey to Atlantis** and **Kraken**. Plan on beginning your second loop at 10:30 a.m., heading early for one of the popular 11:00 a.m. shows, such as **Shamu Adventure**. You can then spend the rest of your day attending the

©2003 SeaWorld of Florida

People who like to go upside down will definitely like Kraken. But why?

scheduled shows in an orderly fashion, visiting the less-crowded attractions that run continuously and working in a meal or two while you're at it.

Running Continuously If you are determined to seek non-animal thrills, there are two rides that you'll want to queue up for quickly when you enter the park. The first of these is **Journey to Atlantis**, a water thrill ride along the lines of Splash Mountain at WDW's Magic Kingdom and Ripsaw Falls at Islands of Adventure. You get very wet on Journey to Atlantis, and this is such a popular concept that the lines at this ride can stretch for 2 hours on busy days. During the winter, if you want to enjoy the ride and still be comfortable during the rest of your day, bring or wear a lightweight rain parka to don during the ride. In summer, either wear a swimsuit under a cover-up, or nylon athletic gear that dries quickly, or bring along a change of clothes. The Minimum Height Requirement (MHR) for Atlantis is 42"/106 cm and children under 48"/122 cm must be accompanied by an adult.

The second thrill ride that thrill riders should put on their morning to-do list is **Kraken**, a ride that makes Journey to Atlantis seem tame. It is one of those new roller coasters that mount guests on a "floorless" vehicle, take them up 15 stories, and twirl them around and upside down 7 times. I confess to having stayed in the viewing area for this one, but my crash dummy volunteers—my sister, Kimberly, and my niece Lena—thought it was just awesome, and they even bought that silly picture of themselves that is taken automatically during one of the drops. The MHR for Kraken is 54"/137 cm.

> This is a good time to mention that there are quite a few **Splash Zones** at SeaWorld where you can get pretty wet. These Splash Zones, well marked at performances, indicate the areas Shamu and the other trained animal performers aim for when they splash water into the audience. Kids seem to especially like this. It's another reason to dress in easily dry-able gear for your visit. Perhaps because of all the splashing and the brevity of clothing involved in modern informal attire, not to mention the heat of the Florida summer, SeaWorld does request that you wear shoes, shirts, and appropriate dress during your visit.

There is a third ride, **Wild Arctic**, you might want to visit early in the day to avoid the crowd, though I wouldn't put it in the thrill ride category. If you've been to the other parks, you'll recognize Wild Arctic as a simulator ride, this one timed to a very beautiful film that puts you in a helicopter over the Arctic. The line splits in two about halfway through the queue: one is for those who want to travel by "air," and the other is for those who want to go by "land." This distinction means only that the "land" travelers see the film without the motion of the simulator. Those with motion sensitivities may want to go by "land," otherwise, take the "air" ride as it is much more fun. MHR

for Arctic is 42"/106 cm and children smaller than 48"/122 cm must be accompanied by a responsible person. (You have one of those in your party, right?)

Following the ride, there is a terrific exhibit of Arctic creatures that you visit via an icy walk-through. The habitats look very realistic, and the creatures—from polar bear to walrus to beluga

©2003 SeaWorld of Florida

Dolphin Cove

whale—are fascinating to see through the glassed-in viewing areas. The exhibit is nice and cold and especially inviting on a summer day.

At **Dolphin Cove**, you'll find one of the experiences that make SeaWorld such a special place. If you are able to stop by this attraction early in the day, you may be able to feed the dolphins. There are cups of sardines for sale nearby, and with cup in hand you can lean right over into the dolphin pool and feed the dolphins yourself. These animals are really smart, and the minute anybody appears by the railing holding a fish, they're over to visit and to snatch it away amidst much laughter. The

park limits the dolphins' intake, so when they've sold something like 20 lbs/9 kg of fish per dolphin, the feeding ends. Having a dolphin come within petting distance is what you've come here for, and this is a great experience. And aren't the folks at SeaWorld smart to have us subsidize their dolphins' chow? Ask if the dolphin nursery is open during your visit. It is always a winner.

©2003 SeaWorld of Florida

At Turtle Point, you'll learn about Florida's endangered sea turtles.

At the nearby **Stingray Lagoon**, you can reach into the pools and touch these interesting creatures. Because of the name of the fish, you'd think this would be dangerous, but it isn't. There is a stingray nursery here that is home to baby stingrays you can also see and touch. Nearby **Turtle Point** should be of particular interest to residents and visitors who want to learn more about Florida's sea turtles. Ninety percent of sea turtle nesting in the United States takes place on the east coast of Florida. Here you can learn about the different species of turtles and see how really large they are. (Depending on the species, sea turtles can range from 250 to 750 lbs/113 to 340 kg.) These are amazing marine reptiles to see up close.

You can see and touch tropical fish, sea urchins, starfish, and anemones at the **Tropical Reef**, adjacent to Turtle Point. All the tanks for these hands-on experiences are at a comfortable height for all but the smallest guests, but reaching the tanks might be a challenge for guests with disabilities who are using wheelchairs or electric vehicles.

Across **Key West Dolphin Stadium** from Turtle Point you'll find the exhibit, **Manatees: The Last Generation?** Scientists now tell us that they have the answer to this question and that if trends continue at their present level, these remarkable creatures will survive on into the future. (You'll find more about the Florida manatee in the Eco-Touring section of this book.) Nevertheless, the 3-D presentation and walk-through at this exhibit explain the challenges faced by manatees. They are the only herbivorous (that is, vegetation-eating) sea going mammals in nature, and nearly all of them in the United States live in Florida's rivers, estuaries, and coastal waters. With the increase in Florida's population, and the increased number of watercraft, manatees have frequent encounters with outboard motors. The only thing you can't get a feel for at this exhibit is how sweet and friendly are these enormous creatures, but there is just no way to show that. All the manatees you'll see in the exhibit have been rescued by SeaWorld's animal rescue team. Those who become healthy enough are returned to their natural environment. This award-winning exhibit is one of the best at SeaWorld.

> **Penguin Encounter** takes you to the South Pole where 6,000 pounds of snow fall daily on more than 200 penguins and puffins. Four species of penguins are featured: king, gentoo, chinstrap, and rockhopper. Guests ride a moving sidewalk through this exhibit, and the scene, at feeding time, is especially lively.

Busch Entertainment Corporation has added one more animal exhibit that has nothing to do with the sea, has everything to do with its brand, and will be much enjoyed by most in your party. At the **Clydesdale Hamlet**, you can watch the staff

©2003 SeaWorld of Florida

The Busch Clydesdales are real show-stoppers.

curry, feed, and otherwise pamper the eight-horse hitch of Clydesdales made famous in Busch beer ads all over the world. The horses parade for photo opportunities at regular intervals, and they can almost always be seen at noon in front of Shamu Stadium. Check the back of your park map for the times and locations of all the Clydesdale appearances.

And speaking of appearances, SeaWorld has created a walk-around Shamu character that signs autographs and poses for photos throughout the day. I didn't see a schedule on the back of the park map for this, so ask a staff member when and where to look for this.

> **Shark Encounter** takes you into a 60-ft tunnel, where you'll see the scary creatures of the deep: eels, barracuda, venomous fish, and sharks. **Pacific Point Preserve** is home to California sea lions and harbor seals. It's a visit to the Monterey Aquarium without the airfare to California.

Scheduled Shows If, upon entering SeaWorld, you have an uncanny precognition that this is your last hour on Planet Earth, hustle over to **Shamu Stadium** and see the **Shamu Adventure** before you pass on to your Great Reward. You absolutely must see this 35-minute performance before you Go. It is SeaWorld's most famous show, featuring its registered trademark. (Shamu was the name of SeaWorld's original orca in San Diego, now long in orca heaven. All the orcas since then travel under the Shamu® moniker.) The show's fame is well-deserved. The young trainers who do the work here are talented, good-looking, and almost upstage the whales. The stadium

©2003 SeaWorld of Florida

seats several thousand people but every seat is a good one, with the Splash Zone seats well marked (the first 14 rows are inside the Zone). We arrived 30 minutes before the show as the guide map suggested and found good seats in the shade. A pre-show on a big-screen television featuring Jack Hanna keeps you entertained while you wait.

Right up there in the sea mammal entertainment pantheon is **Key West Dolphin Fest**, presented on the other side of the park from the Shamu Adventure at the **Key West Dolphin Stadium**. This 20-minute show features dolphins jumping, splashing, diving, and dancing on their tails on cue. Mid-show, trainers bring in some very large, very strange-looking creatures called false killer whales and these have also been trained in an amazing way. The ones I saw on a recent visit were called Shadow, Streak, and Storm, and as big as they were, they moved as gracefully as the dolphins. **Shamu Adventure** and **Key West Dolphin Fest** together are worth the price of admission. Yet

there are six more scheduled daytime shows to take in and two nighttime spectaculars still on the docket.

Clyde and Seamore Take Pirate Island is performed at the **Sea Lion and Otter Stadium**, adjacent to Pacific Point Preserve. The name of this enjoyable romp changes from year to year, but it always involves a comedy hunt for some kind of lost treasure, and there is something pleasantly vaudevillian about

©2003 SeaWorld of Florida
Clyde and Seamore Take Pirate Island

it (Arf! Arf!). It is 30 minutes long, and once again it is a good idea to come 20 to 30 minutes before the scheduled show time so that you can get a good seat in or out of the shade and in or out of the Splash Zone, depending on your preferences.

Pets Ahoy! features cats, dogs, birds, and even a pig at the **Seaport Theater** in SeaWorld's new **WaterFront**. Most of the animals in this 25-minute show were rescued from animal shelters. If you think it isn't possible to train your cat, remain at the WaterFront for **Kat 'n' Kaboodle**, a street show performed by both wild and domesticated felines. Since the show is out-of-doors, it can be cancelled during bad weather, so the earlier in the day you can see it the better (thunderstorms generally come in the late afternoon).

Finally, **Odyssea** is the latest version of SeaWorld's Cirque-like modern circus. I'm not a big fan of the original Cirque, so I can take this or leave it alone, but I know a lot of people like this sort of thing. The 30-minute show is performed at the **Nautilus**

Theater, located between the Shark Encounter and the Clydesdale Hamlet. Can you see what I mean when I say there is an awful lot to see at this park in just one day?

When your mind becomes boggled by too many shows, slip over to the **Arcade** and **Games Area** (for the older family members) or next door to **Shamu's Happy Harbor** (for the younger family members) and feel free to lose yourself in a little playtime. The landmark **Sky Tower** costs a few dollars extra per person, but provides you with a great view of SeaWorld and the surrounding area. The new flamingo-shaped **Paddle Boats** are fun to climb into for a quiet break on the lagoon, but you must be at least 56"/142 cm to ride the paddle boats alone. There is one more spot, not highlighted on your map, that provides you with a great place to take a break: between Turtle Point and the Friends of the Wild gift shop, there is a lovely little park. Beautifully landscaped with begonias, cyclamen, and other subtropical plants, it is a shady spot to sit and relax. My family especially enjoyed the rich Florida vegetation that surrounds you here.

©2003 SeaWorld of Florida
Shamu's Happy Harbor is a playground.

If you have managed to pace yourself and plan to stay on into the evening, **Shamu Rocks America** awaits you at Shamu Stadium. It is a louder version of the traditional Shamu show, performed in the evening hours. **Fireworks at the WaterFront** is the show that winds up the day. Make sure you're across the bridge between Shamu Stadium and the WaterFront 30 minutes before closing time, as the bridge closes for the evening before the fireworks begin. You can still get out of the park going the other way, but it is a longer walk, and at this point I am going to assume you're just a wee bit tired. Still and all, I know you've had a good time. SeaWorld is a great park, very different from the other two major league attractions in Orlando.

DISCOVERY COVE ORLANDO

W hen somebody told me about this place, and how pricey it was, I figured it would be a tough sell, which shows you just how much I don't know about the entertainment business. Discovery Cove is so popular, in spite of its price, that it sometimes has a waiting list of people who want to get in. Visiting Discovery Cove is like spending one day at a luxury tropical resort. The park is beautiful, there is a surplus of staff, and you have the option of sitting by the pool with a cool drink in your hand or taking part in a dolphin swim and snorkeling adventures. The big difference between this and a fancy resort hotel is that you don't check into a room and spend the night here. Discovery Cove is open 365 days a year from 9:00 a.m. to 5:30 p.m.

Pockets Full of Miracles The price for a 1-day ticket to Discovery Cove (2003 prices) is $179 per person, plus tax, with no discounts except for very small children. The price does include lunch and a 7-day pass to SeaWorld, so if you deduct those benefits—which you may be laying out cash for anyway—it brings your cost per person for the day to about $100. Drinks are not included in the price. Children under 6 years of age are not allowed to take part in the

©2003 SeaWorld of Florida
The dolphin swim is the highlight of the Discovery Cove experience.

©2003 SeaWorld of Florida

Encounters with sea life make Discovery Cove especially interesting.

dolphin swim (so there is a reduction in price for them), and children under 3 years of age get in free.

Limited Engagement Attendance is limited to 1,000 guests each day at this 30-acre park. If you can spring for the premium ticket price, this will be one of your rare, uncrowded adventures in Orlando.

Locale Discovery Cove Orlando is directly across the road (the access road that is) from SeaWorld. See the directions to SeaWorld on the earlier pages and follow them to Discovery Cove. Turn left into Discovery Cove rather than turning right into SeaWorld.

World Full of Wonder Each visitor can reserve a time to swim with the bottlenose dolphins at Discovery Cove, and this, understandably, is the reason most people come to the park. The ticket includes unlimited access to the Coral Reef, the Ray Lagoon, the resort pool, Tropical River, and the Aviary. Parking is included, along with any snorkeling equipment, wet suits, towels, and other diving paraphernalia you might need.

Aviary If you swim under the waterfall you'll enter a series of free-flight aviaries. The birds are accustomed to people so you can touch, feed, and otherwise interact with them. Park staff members stand by to tell you about the species and answer your questions.

Coral Reef, Tropical River, Ray Lagoon Busch Entertainment has created these artificial grottos and stocked them with beautiful, safe, interesting creatures for visitors to view as they snorkel. As part of your ticket, you can swim as much as you like in these areas.

Buffet Lunch This is provided at the Laguna Grill, but you'll have to spring for your own Bud (or Pepsi) in spite of the corporate relationship between this park and Anheuser-Busch, Inc.

Faster Than Lightning If you choose to swim with the dolphins, the experience accounts for 90 minutes of your daylong visit. There is a 30-minute orientation for the groups of one to two dozen guests that will be sharing the adventure. The staff stands by and handles this part of the day very carefully to make sure neither the dolphins nor the bipeds get frightened or in any way have a bad experience. At the end of the hour, the dolphins give the guests "rides" to the shore. Hang on!

Reservations and Information Since attending Discovery Cove is more like going to a resort than a theme park, reservations are recommended. Call **877-434-7268** or **407-370-1280** (for international callers). You can also make reservations on line at www.discoverycove.com.

©2003 SeaWorld of Florida
Whether you visit SeaWorld or Discovery Cove, you may want to end your day at the WaterFront.

K-20—Business District, Kissimmee, Fla.

MORE ATTRACTIONS

B eyond the Walt Disney World Resort, Universal Studios, and SeaWorld, there are many, many smaller, what you might call "professional vacation attractions" designed for Central Florida visitors. The best way to learn about these other attractions is to contact the people in the business of promoting Central Florida vacations. Like the best things in life, their help is free.

The Orlando/Orange County Convention and Visitors Bureau This is a clearinghouse of information on the region. Every major hotel, attraction, restaurant and tourist service belongs to the CVB. That makes it possible for the CVB to help you book hotel rooms, buy attraction tickets, and generally plan your visit in advance.

The Orlando/Orange County Convention and Visitors Bureau
6700 Forum Drive, Orlando, Florida 32821
Free Visitors Kit **800-646-2087**
Questions (Between 8:00 a.m. and 7:00 p.m.) **407-363-5872**
http://orlandoinfo.com

The City of Orlando If you want to know more about the city itself, you can get information on everything from voter registration to a schedule of the city's annual events.

Orlando City Hall, One City Commons, 400 South Orange Avenue, P.O. Box 4990,
Orlando, Florida 32802-4990
www.ci.orlando.fl.us **407-246-2121**

Orlando Regional Chamber of Commerce This is the largest business organization in Central Florida, and it is the place to go for any contacts you need to make regarding Central Florida commerce and economics.
75 South Ivanhoe Boulevard, Orlando, Florida 32804
www.orlando.org **407-425-1234**

Kissimmee-St. Cloud Convention and Visitors Bureau Kissimmee-St. Cloud is closer to Walt Disney World than is the City of Orlando, and a lot of visitors stay within its borders. Just remember to pronounce it Kah-SIM-eee, except at night when you can say "KISS-a-mee," as long as you don't mind the consequences.
Kissimmee-St. Cloud Convention and Visitors Bureau
P.O. Box 422007, Kissimmee, Florida 34742
www.floridakiss.com **800-333-KISS**

Seminole County Convention and Visitor's Bureau This is the county of eco-touring and the county's tourism web site reflects this emphasis.
www.visitseminole.com **407-665-2900**

Brevard County The "Space Coast" is the home of NASA launches and stunningly beautiful beaches and Port Canaveral.
www.space-coast.com .... **800-93-Ocean (800-936-2326)**

Daytona Beach Area Convention and Visitors Bureau Spring-breakers, bike-weekers, speed-weekers, and fans of the "Fun Coast" can check the Daytona Beach Area CVB Web site for temperature, beach conditions, and surf temperature any time of the day or night.
www.daytonabeach.org **800-854-1234**

22 LOTS HERE

LAKE EMMA

28 LOTS HERE

BAYLARIAN · SUBDIVISION
Comprising about 50 remaining Lots at this locati
South and East of Orange County Hospital at City Li
Numbers indicate location of following Residences and
1. Grocery Store   3. DR. STAFFORD   6. J.F. HANSEN   11. PR
2. J. BAYLARIAN   4. L.H. YOHEM   9. H. DOBSON   12. PR
3. F.V. BAYLARIAN   6. J.B. HAUSKERW.   8. R.J. HOLLINBECK   12. PR

O-98   AIRPLANE VIEW OF BUSINESS SECTION, SHOW

N-M-D AIR PHOTO, ORLANDO

3A-H

"BEAUTIFUL"

Delan

THE CITY BEAUTIFUL

O-112—Orlando Air Base, Orlando, Fla.

O. 21

Orlando

FLORIDA

"The City Beautiful"

O-26—Bird's-Eye View of Tropical Lake Eola Park and Band Shell, Orlando, Fla. "The City Beautiful"

There have been four different bandstands at Lake Eola. The first lasted from 1918 to 1924; the second (seen above in 1942) was in place from 1924 to 1957; the third, from 1962 to 1986; followed by the amphitheater in place today.

ORLANDO'S FIRST PARK

In 1873, Jacob Summerlin, one of Orlando's earliest residents, bought 200 acres of rural land right in the center of what is now downtown Orlando. Summerlin was a cattleman, and at the heart of his land was a small lake that local residents called Sandy Beach Lake. It wasn't the best-looking place, and its shores were so boggy after a rain that if cattle wandered into the bog it was not uncommon for them to disappear entirely. Summerlin's son Bob must have liked it though, as the lake was renamed Eola in honor of his fiancée[1], who died of typhoid a week before their planned wedding day. In 1883, old Jacob Summerlin gave Lake Eola and a small surrounding right-of-way to the City of Orlando to be used for a park. He stipulated that the property would revert to the Summerlin family if it were not improved and used in this way. Today, more than 1 million people visit Lake Eola each year, making it not only Orlando's first park, but also its most popular.

The park is at 195 North Rosalind Avenue in downtown Orlando. Open 5:00 a.m. to sunset 365 days a year. For more information, log on to www.cityoforlando.net.

---

[1] Some sources say Eola was his wife, some say she was a family friend. Kena Fries says she was his fiancée.

Big Tree Park
FROM LITTLE ACORNS

ere is a small park devoted to a large tree. The 500-year-old Southern live oak (Quercus virginiana) is the oldest and largest live oak within the Orlando city limits. Its branches cover more than half of the 0.7-acre park, creating lots of shade for visitors. In 2000, the city and a team of residents worked on improvements to Big Tree Park, which now include benches and seats carved by a chainsaw artist (great idea, but FYI they hold water after a rain), new lighting for the spectacular tree, and new signage. The tree, in the Lake Highland neighborhood of Orlando, is certainly worth seeing. It was an acorn about the time Columbus set sail for America.

The park is open from 5:00 a.m. to sunset. Though the tree is beautifully lighted at night, it is much more impressive during the day, when you can really see its size. 930 North Thornton Avenue. Thornton is just a block from Route 17-92, about a quarter of a mile off Colonial Drive. Directions can be found on the city's Web site at www.cityoforlando.net.

A vintage postcard (1911), not of Orlando's tree, but it could be. Orlando's is about this size, maybe slightly larger.

Pioneers say there used to be a huge live oak like this one near Fort Gatlin, just south of what is now downtown Orlando. It was called Council Oak because tradition said Seminole warriors held councils under its branches. That tree was struck by lightning and burned about 1888, according to long-time Orlando resident Kena Fries (1867-1945).

HENRY P. LEU GARDENS

ere is a treat smack in the middle of one of Orlando's prettiest neighborhoods. The Henry P. Leu Gardens began as a homestead in the late 1850s, when David and Angeline Mizell took ownership of the property. Their son built a farmhouse here, and then two more owners succeeded the Mizells until Henry P. Leu bought the property in 1936. Leu was an Orlando native who was brilliant in business and spent much of his early life proving it. In middle age, the eligible bachelor finally married, and it was for his wife that Henry Leu purchased the home and 40 acres that now make up the gardens. The couple traveled the world to bring back plants for their garden, and it became such a showplace that the Leus invited the public to drive through the property and enjoy it in all seasons. In 1961, Henry Leu sold the house and gardens to the City of Orlando for a living botanical museum.

Because that was Mr. Leu's wish, the city is careful not to identify Leu Gardens as a recreational facility. There is no picnicking, for example, and no pets, bikes, or skateboards are allowed. However, if you are a garden fancier you will find it full of treats.

Mr. and Mrs. Henry P. Leu with their dogs, and at right, the Henry P. Leu house.

Twelve full-time gardeners maintain the landscaping for the public. There are gardens of herbs, roses, annuals, perennials, tropical plants, and the largest collection of camellias east of the Rockies—and that is just to name a few of the kinds of "garden varieties" within the property. The historic Leu House is open each day from 10:00 a.m. to 3:30 p.m. for 30-minute tours.

The new garden house on Lake Rowena, which also has a gift shop, is the site of many weddings and wedding receptions each year. It is also where Leu Gardens holds a full schedule of gardening classes. Three times a year there are special evening walks, during which picnics are allowed. And here's the best tip of all: Mr. Leu wanted to make sure everyone could enjoy his garden; so, even though it is not widely publicized, the entrance fee is waived on Monday mornings from 9:00 a.m. until noon.

*Take I-4 Exit 85 (Princeton Street) and drive east. Princeton reaches a dead end at Mills, also known as Route 17-92. Turn right onto Mills, then left onto Virginia, then left again onto Forest. The left turn into Leu Gardens from Forest is very well marked. Open every day of the year from 9:00 a.m. to 5:00 p.m., except Christmas Day and during the month of July. Small admission price. Tours are available if you call ahead to the Education Department, **407-246-3621** or **407-246-3669**. The general number is **407-246-2620**. www.leugardens.org.*

You'll see remotely-controlled miniature sailboats on Loch Haven twice each week.

LOCH HAVEN PARK

Orlando's Loch Haven is home to herons, egrets, and other exotic subtropical wildlife. Adjacent Loch Haven Cultural Park is designed to be the center of Orlando's cultural life, in a complex with excellent variety, great parking, and easy access.

Loch Haven Cultural Park is at 777 East Princeton, Orlando. North of downtown Orlando between Orange Avenue and Route 17-92. Take Exit 85 off I-4 (Princeton). Go east 1/2 mile on Princeton, and follow the signs.

The Orlando Science Center This is a cooperative venture between the City of

The skywalk at the Orlando Science Center.

Orlando and the Orlando public schools. It is a first rate—and very entertaining— science center with a planetarium, an observatory, two giant-screen theaters, and exhibits to interest all ages. If some of the techniques used here and even the exhibit names seem reminiscent of Innoventions at Epcot, it is only because they are in fact somewhat similar. For a much-lower-than-Disney price you can enjoy TechWorld and BodyZone, Science City and 123 Math Avenue, NatureWorks and Wired Science, and save time for planetarium shows about galaxy collisions and black hole mysteries. The Darden Adventure Theater and the Dr. Phillips CineDome run giant-screen films and, better yet, give everybody in the family a chance to sit down. (I know I say this a lot, but I'm trying to help you pace yourself!)

Park on the same side as the Mennello Museum of American Folk Art (off Princeton) and walk over to the Science Center on the 2nd-floor skywalk. Ticket prices depend on what you want to see, but fees are very reasonable. Open Tuesday-Thursday, 9:00 a.m. to 5:00 p.m.; Friday and Saturday, 9:00 a.m. to 9:00 p.m.; Sunday, noon to 5:00 p.m. Closed Monday, except for school holidays. **407-514-2000**. www.osc.org.

"New England Autumn" by Earl Cunningham

The Mennello Museum of American Folk Art Folk art has grown increasingly hip, but Michael and Marilyn Mennello were collecting long before the fashions came. The heart of their collection is Earl Cunningham's (1893-1977) extraordinary work, which Mrs. Mennello began collecting when she was just a student. Pictures of his paintings don't do them justice. You will be wowed by his colors when you see them in the museum. Other exhibits rotate. This is a very small facility, so a visit here can be squeezed in even when time is short. As you leave the museum look to your right—not a hard right, but at about 2 o'clock from your right shoulder. You'll see a huge Southern live oak tree—one of the biggest in the city outside "Big Tree Park." Walk over to it and read the plaque in front of the tree and you'll learn more about this ancient oak.

Open Tuesday-Saturday, 11:00 a.m. to 5:00 p.m., Sunday, noon to 5:00 p.m. Closed Mondays and major holidays. Small entrance donation. **407-246-4278**. www.mennellomuseum.com.

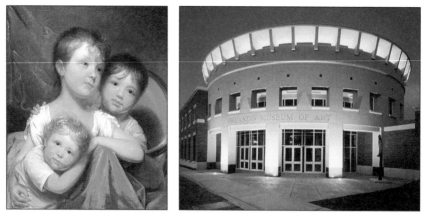

"Portrait of Three Children" by Rembrandt Peale (1778-1806) is one of a collection of paintings on long-term loan to the Orlando Museum of Art from The Martin Andersen-Gracia Andersen Foundation. At right, a wing of the newly-expanded museum.

The Orlando Museum of Art This museum was expanded for the turn of the 21st century and now hosts exhibits from around the world. It has a busy and popular series of events and activities including gallery talks, "Sunday Afternoons in the Park," lectures, and "First Thursdays," which are monthly mix-and-mingle social events. Check the Web site or call for information on current exhibits and events.

This is on the opposite side of Princeton Street from the Mennello Museum. Park off Princeton or off Rollins, depending on availability. Small entrance donation. Open Tuesday-Friday, 10:00 a.m. to 4:00 p.m., Saturday and Sunday, noon to 4:00 p.m. Closed Mondays and major holidays. **407-896-4231**. www.omart.org.

Orlando-UCF Shakespeare Theater This repertory theater premiered in the spring of 1989 at the Lake Eola Amphitheater with alternating performances of two Shakespeare plays—a tragedy and a comedy—a tradition that continues to delight audiences. Though Lake Eola remains its primary venue, in 2001, the new $3.5 million John and Rita Lowndes Shakespeare Center opened at Loch Haven Park across from the Orlando Museum of Art. It includes the Marilyn and Sig Goldman Theater, with 118 seats, and the Ken and Trish Mageson Theater, about twice that size. The schedule has expanded beyond Shakespeare to the traditional, the modern, and the experimental. This is a professional theater that hosts many Equity actors. It is known for its innovative take on the Bard, and its fabulous costumes. Check the Web site or telephone for a performance schedule and ticket information.

812 East Rollins Street, Orlando. Across from the Orlando Museum of Art. Box office is open Monday-Friday, 10:00 a.m. to 5:00 p.m. **407-447-1700**. *www.shakespearefest.org.*

Fire Department, Orlando, Fla.—38

An early Orlando fire station. The postcard is from the collection of Russell V. Hughes.

The Orlando Fire Museum This is a dandy little museum in Orlando's Fire Station #3, built in 1926. In 1978, the old station was moved to the grounds of Loch Haven Park from its original home near the corner of Dade and College Streets. Several agencies joined with the Orange County Historical Society (now the Historical Society of Central Florida) to restore it, and it opened as a museum in 1985. Inside you'll find an 1885 horse-drawn fire cart, a 1908 horse-drawn steam pumper, and a 1915 American La France, Orlando's first motorized fire engine. The original brass sliding pole was cut into pieces and given to firemen as souvenirs, but a new one has been added and a piece of the old one is on display. When the Historical Society moved from Loch Haven to downtown Orlando, the fire house couldn't move with it—moving it once was tough enough. So it remains in the courtyard of what is now the headquarters of the Orlando-UCF Shakespeare Theater and is operated by the Orlando Fire Department.

Open Tuesdays and Thursdays, 9:00 a.m. to 1:00 p.m., at Loch Haven Park. Open on other days by special appointment. Call Amron Jones at **407-246-2390**. *Park on the Orlando Museum of Art side of Loch Haven and walk to the front entrance of the Orlando-UCF Shakespeare Center. The Orlando Fire Museum is in the courtyard ahead.*

HERITAGE SQUARE

H eritage Square is the 1-acre park in downtown Orlando directly in front of the 1927 Orange County Courthouse. A courthouse annex was removed and the old courthouse was remodeled to make it the home of the Orange County Regional History Center. The new courthouse—completed in 1997—is just up Orange Avenue a couple of blocks.

The Orange County Regional History Center In 2000, this center for local history moved to its new location from its former cozy home at Loch Haven Park. By remodeling the old courthouse, the Historical Society of Central Florida preserved a landmark building and provided itself with lots of room for expansion. Now the center offers 35,000 square feet of historic exhibits that take the visitor back 12,000 years. It includes an orientation theater, permanent and rotating exhibits, and an excellent research library. The Historium gift shop offers great Floridiana.

The Orange County Regional History Center (above) and a vintage postcard (top) of the 1927 courthouse in which the Center has now found a home.

65 East Central Boulevard, Orlando, Florida. Open Monday-Saturday, 10:00 a.m. to 5:00 p.m., Sunday, noon to 5:00 p.m. Closed on Thanksgiving Day, Christmas Eve, Christmas Day, New Year's Eve, and New Year's Day. Take Exit 82C, Anderson Street, off I-4. Turn right onto Anderson to Magnolia Avenue and turn left. Take Magnolia to Central Boulevard and turn right onto Central, then right again into the parking garage across from the Library. The History Center is just one block away. Small admission fee. **407-836-8500**. www.thehistorycenter.org.

This is a postcard from Bamboo Groves where visitors were welcomed by the sign: "Please help yourself. Eat 'til it hurts." From the collection of Russell V. Hughes.

Farmers Market at Heritage Square   Orlando has been operating its Saturday morning Farmers Market since 1989, though the venue recently changed to Heritage Square—in front of the Orange County Regional History Center. Here you'll find organic vegetables, home-baked pastries, fresh coffee, herbs, orchids, soaps, and—a recent addition—crafts. Pets on leash are welcome. Take note of the sculpture in the square of the man in a big hat wrestling an alligator. The sculpture is modeled on a picture in the Orange County Regional History Center archives. The sculpture identifies the man as Bunk Baxter, and Bunk Baxter did exist, and he did wrestle gators. But, no one is really sure if that was BB in the archival photograph. It makes a good sculpture though!

There is free parking at the lot on the northeast corner of Magnolia Avenue and Washington Street; at the Library Parking Garage just one block away at 112 East Central Boulevard (take your ticket with you to the market and get it validated); and at lots on South Court Avenue, south of Pine Street. The market is open every Saturday from 8:00 a.m. until 2:30 p.m. **407-246-2555**. *See the directions on the previous page to the Orange County Regional History Center. The Farmers Market is directly in front of the OCRHC.*

Nicer Than Its Name

THE ORLANDO CENTROPLEX

The Orlando Centroplex is a group of public facilities just on the west side of I-4. It includes a theater, a baseball field, an exposition center, an indoor sports arena, and a football stadium. These facilities feature concerts, plays, expos, and sporting events.

Go on line to www.orlandocentroplex.com for schedules. Or call **407-849-2001** for event information, and **407-849-2020** for ticket information. Take I-4 to Exit 83 and follow the signs. It is often easier in the evening to park in nearby downtown Orlando and walk to Centroplex events than to find parking at the site.

The Citrus Bowl Built in 1936, this football stadium has been expanded and modernized three times in the intervening years. It plays host to the annual New Year's Day football classic, as well as to University of Central Florida and Jones High School games. Performers such as the Rolling Stones, Paul McCartney, and Elton John have played this stadium, and there is always a full schedule of annual concerts. Legend has it that the land on which this stadium was built was once a dumping ground for rotten citrus—and that is one of the stories of how the bowl got its name.

The Orlando Magic of the NBA play at the TD Waterhouse Centre.

TD Waterhouse Centre Home of the NBA's Orlando Magic, this indoor arena also features Orlando Seals hockey and Orlando Predators arena football. Jimmy Buffett plays a concert here almost every year. Eat sparingly before you attend anything at TDWC: the seats are not exactly spacious.

Robert S. Carr Performing Arts Centre The "Bob Carr" is home to the Orlando Broadway Series and other theatrical, musical, dance, and cultural events.

The Expo Centre This is a relatively small exposition center where business conferences and expositions are held.

ORLANDO, FLORIDA; THE CITY BEAUTIFUL. 35

CINCINNATI REDS TRAINING ON TINKER FIELD, ORLANDO, FLA.

Cincinnati Reds training on Tinker Field. From the collection of Russell V. Hughes.

Tinker Field Orlando historians say baseball has been played at Tinker Field—at least on the spot where Tinker Field now stands—since 1914. The field is named after Joseph Bert Tinker, Hall of Fame player for the Chicago Cubs (1902-1912) and member of the Tinker-to-Evers-to-Chance double-play combination made famous in a poem by columnist Franklin P. Adams.[2] Tinker came to Orlando in 1921 as owner of the minor league Orlando Gulls, and the stadium was built about 1923. In 1963, the old grandstands were torn down and new ones installed—the best-known features of which are the ceiling fans on the overhang, which make every effort to move the sultry air of an Orlando summer night. The Cubs, Dodgers, and Senators all had spring training here at various times, and several Florida League and Southern League teams made their homes at Tinker over the years. In 2003, the City of Orlando applied to place Tinker Field on the National Register of Historic Places. Tinker Field remains in the shadow of the Citrus Bowl, waiting for someone to shout: "Play ball!"

If you can get in for a tour, look for the statue of Clark Griffith, once the majority owner of the Washington Senators, inside the gate. Griffith brought the Senators to Tinker Field for spring training in 1936, and this boost in the midst of the Depression left Orlando very grateful to him. Call the Centroplex public relations office with questions: **407-849-2001.** *www.orlandocentroplex.com*

---

[2] The poem is called "Baseball's Sad Lexicon" and begins:
"*These are the saddest of possible words: 'Tinker to Evers to Chance ...' "*
The words were sad because Adams was a fan of the New York Giants and he hated it when his Giants hit into a double-play!

DUBSDREAD GOLF COURSE

D ubsdread is a City of Orlando 18-hole public golf course, with an interesting history. Orlando entrepreneur Carl Dann came up with the idea for Dubsdread in 1923 after he had some sort of "fuss" one weekend at the Orlando Country Club. The following Monday, Dann buttonholed everyone he knew and asked each for $1,000 to help him build a new country club. He bought what had been a hog farm in the College Park section of Orlando, developed the golf course, and subdivided the land around the course for home sites. All his investors made a profit and became charter members of the new club, which he called Dubsdread because it was, as historian Eve Bacon writes, " … a difficult course, and dreaded by 'dubs,' or unskilled players." Carl Dann's son, Carl Dann II, was a five-time Florida Amateur Champion who ran the club from 1931 until his death in 1970. He inaugurated the Orlando Open, which attracted the likes of Sam Snead, Bobby Jones, and Ben Hogan. The clubhouse served as a club during World War II for flyers training to go overseas. Orlando PGA star David Peoples retrieved balls at Dubsdread as a kid. In 1978, the Dann family sold the club to the City of Orlando to keep the land from being subdivided. Play the course, and let us know if Dubsdread remains true to its name.

Open daily 7:00 a.m. to sunset at 549 West Par Street, Orlando. Take Exit 86, Par Street, off I-4. Go west on Par. The clubhouse is on the north side of the street. The historic clubhouse has been re-done and has a full bar and restaurant, run by local operators, and the food and service are excellent. Take a minute to look at the old photos on the clubhouse walls. **407-246-2551.**

O. 115—Beautiful Dubsdread Country Club, Orlando, Fla.

A Park Scene in Florida

TENNIS, FISHING, SWIMMING, BIKING, BOATING, PICNICKING ANYONE?

T *he City of Orlando has 83 public parks encompassing 2,150 acres. This includes 21 lakeside parks, eight special facilities, and two senior centers.*

There are parks with public swimming pools, such as the **Princeton Park and College Park Pool**, at Helen Avenue and Rugby Street, and parks with public tennis courts, including the **Orlando Tennis Center**, 649 West Livingston. There are parks set aside for competitive sports, among them the **West Colonial Soccer/Rugby Fields** at 4400 West Colonial Drive. **Turkey Lake Park**, 3401 South Hiawassee Road, is known as the place to go for group picnics and outdoor gatherings.

For cyclists (as well as hikers and rollerbladers), Orlando has the **Cady Way Bike Trail**, with parking at the north end of the trail at Winter Park's Cady Way Pool, and at the south end of the trail too, near Orlando's Fashion Square Mall. The 3.8-mile trail is paved and has drinking fountains and places to rest along the route—but make a note that the only restrooms you'll find are at the Cady Way Pool. The trail is open from sunrise to sunset, and riding the trail definitely beats dodging those SUVs that zoom along all our roadways these days. For more information, call **407-836-6160**.

To review all of the available Orlando park facilities, log on to www.cityoforlando.net and surf to the section on parks. Most parks can be reserved by calling **407-246-2287**. *For Lake Eola and Turkey Lake Park, call* **407-246-2288**.

Jack Kerouac in Residence
HIP TO BE SQUARE

Writer Jack Kerouac (1922-1969) once lived in Orlando, and the house he lived in still stands. Most people wouldn't connect somewhat-square Orlando with this literary light of the Beat Generation. But the author of *On the Road* was never quite the New York hipster he was made out to be. He was born Jean-Louis de Kerouac in Lowell, Massachusetts. He wrangled a football scholarship to Columbia University, but instead of studying, he hooked up with a Greenwich Village crowd that included Allen Ginsberg, William S. Burroughs, and Neal Cassady. Cassady—a handsome, hard-drinking, drug-using charmer—became one of Kerouac's best friends. They took several cross-country trips together, and these

became the basis for Kerouac's novel *On the Road*, famously written on one long roll of paper. Cassady—called Dean Moriarty in *On the Road*—must have been quite a character. Before his death in 1968, he figured prominently in another important book—*The Electric Kool-Aid Acid Test* by Tom Wolfe. But I digress.

1418 Clouser Avenue, Orlando

On the Road was scheduled for publication in September 1957. In July, Kerouac joined his mother in a small rented home at 1418 Clouser Avenue in the College Park neighborhood of Orlando. In September, he took a break to go to New York for the release of *On the Road*, and he returned to Orlando in October. In the little cottage, he sat down and wrote *The Dharma Bums*, a book still considered one of his best. By April, he had moved on. He didn't live in the house a long time, but then he didn't live anywhere for long.

In the late 1990s, television reporter Bob Kealing uncovered the Kerouac association to the house. He and others began the Kerouac Project, which set up a foundation to buy the home, and which now operates a writer-in-residence program allowing qualified writers to live there for three months at a time, rent free. The house is now an Orlando Historic Landmark.

There are tours of the house from time to time. Contact the Kerouac Project, P.O. Box 747477, Orlando, Florida 32854, or call **407-841-1228** *for information. Or, log on to www.kerouacproject.org.*

Orlando's City Hall
MEL GIBSON, ART GALLERIES, AND A FRONT PORCH

Orlando's city hall is a beautiful, modern structure at 400 South Orange Avenue, opened June 1, 1991. The previous city hall, built in 1958, was left in place on the adjacent lot while city officials moved to the new building. Then, in the early morning hours of October 25, 1991, the old building was imploded, an event filmed in 35 millimeter and used in the opening sequences of the movie *Lethal Weapon 3*.

This could allow everyone in Orlando to claim fewer than six degrees of separation from Mel Gibson—if that's what everyone should want to do.

The new building had another brush with greatness. During the 1994 World Cup games in Orlando, the domed roof of city hall was covered to look like a huge soccer ball. Well, I said it was a brush, not a collision.

Art at City Hall Orlando made a commitment to public art with the opening of the new structure. Thanks to the talented Frank Holt (also Director/Curator of the Mennello Museum) there are now two art galleries within city hall. The first is the **Terrace Gallery**, which is on the first floor and can be accessed without going through all the new government security required post-9/11. It has rotating exhibits of Florida artists and is open Monday-Friday, 7:00 a.m. to 9:00 p.m., as well as Saturday and Sunday, noon to 5 p.m. On the third floor, the **Mayor's Gallery** frequently features shows devoted to a single artist and to the city's growing collection of Florida folk art.

Visiting the Mayor's Gallery does require going through security. It is open Monday-Friday, 8:00 a.m. to 5:00 p.m. Both galleries are free.

Rockin' The plaza in front of city hall, called City Hall Commons, has fountains, trees, and lots of wooden benches for relaxing in the shade. Its most charming features are the rocking chairs on city hall's "front porch." The building is almost military in bearing: the rockers add a homey, comfortable contrast.

Photos on this page by Gene Randall

Downtown Orlando
Walking and Driving Tour

Oops! This is really Orange Avenue looking south. From the collection of Russell V. Hughes.

A Tour for Walking and Driving
HISTORIC DOWNTOWN ORLANDO

Orlando began as a small city with Lake Eola at its center. As a consequence, the downtown and the most historic district of the city surround the lake. This tour is designed to reveal some of the old and some of the new in Orlando's downtown, and on into the pretty neighborhood of Thornton Park, on Lake Eola's east side. It is 2.8 miles from the starting point to the garage at which I definitely think you should leave your car behind. But you can park your car and walk any part of this route. To find the starting point, exit I-4 at Colonial Drive (Exit 83B) going east, and find the corner of Colonial and Orange Avenue. When you do, turn south onto Orange, which is one way heading south.

Pull over to the right side of the road into one of the parking spaces available on this block of Orange Avenue and let your car idle for a minute. In the first block on your right, is a large empty lot (**#1**). This is where the **Orange Court Hotel** once stood. Built in the early 1920s, the hotel had a large neon sign that was a landmark in downtown Orlando. It was torn down in 1988, and it is sad to see that nothing has gone up on the lot.

While you sit, look to your left and you'll see the building housing the *Orlando Sentinel* (**#2**), Orlando's daily newspaper. The **Fort Gatlin Hotel**, which opened

THE HOTEL FORT GATLIN — ORLANDO, FLORIDA

The Fort Gatlin Hotel was demolished to make room for a printing plant.

in 1926, once stood on the southern end of that site. In 1946, the *Orlando Morning Sentinel* and the *Orlando Star* had a warehouse built on the northern part of the site. In 1964, the newspapers bought the hotel and tore it down to make room for a larger printing plant. The clock you see on the building once stood in front of Gus Lawton's Jewelry Store on Orange Avenue, and then in front of Happy Jack's Used Cars. It was installed here and put into working order in 1951.

If you decide to continue by automobile, ease it into traffic, and at the corner of Orange and Concord Street look to your right. The **Firestone Tire and Rubber Company** building (**#3**), constructed in 1928-1929, was Firestone's headquarters in Orlando until 1977. As you cross Amelia Street, look left and you'll see the new **Orange County Courthouse (#4)**. This is the seventh county courthouse in downtown Orlando since the city was named county seat in the 1850s. Several of the early buildings burned down. One that was built in 1927 remains, and you'll see it later on the tour. This one was completed in 1997. At Livingston Street, turn right, but be careful: *the hard right turn is for buses only*, so turn right *after* the median and drive to **100 West Livingston Street (#5)**, where you can turn around in the adjacent parking lot. This building, constructed in 1900, was used to repair railroad boilers and then was purchased by Henry P. Leu, who made fire extinguishers here. Leu built the fabulous Leu Gardens, now a city park.

Return to Orange Avenue on Livingston the way you came. Turn right onto Orange Avenue and move into the left lane. As you approach Washington Street, look left to the southeast corner of the intersection for **65 North Orange Avenue (#6)**. This distinctive building once was the home of **Rutland's**, a men's clothing store, and though the business is gone, the building remains.

Ahead on your right, you'll see the marquee of a movie theater. There are a couple of places to park out front, and if you can, pull into one of them. This building was constructed in 1921 as the **Beacham Theater (#7)**, which first hosted vaudeville acts and later become Orlando's first movie theater. Across the street is the **Angebilt Hotel (#8)**, now converted into office space. The Angebilt was Orlando's first "skyscraper," one of its finest hotels during the land boom of the 1920s. There used to be a tunnel under the street that went from the Angebilt to the Beacham, so performers could get into the theater without being seen by patrons.

At the intersection of Orange and Central Boulevard on the right or southwest corner, look for the old **Dickson-Ives Department Store (#9)**, with its terracotta friezes above you on the building's façade. Dickson and Ives had a grocery store here beginning in the 1880s. They built this structure when they began operating as a department store in 1920—back when we all used to go "downtown" to shop. The department store flourished for 45 years, but went out of business in 1965.

Next, you will be turning left on Pine Street (which is one way, going east). At the intersection of Orange and Pine on the northwest corner (your right-hand side) is the **O'Connell Building (#10)** (32-38 South Orange Avenue). This building went

Rutland's was Orlando's best known men's store.
Both of the postcards on these two pages are from the collection of Russell V. Hughes.

up in 1886, replacing the Magnolia Hotel, and there are not too many buildings of this age remaining downtown.

Now turn left on Pine Street. As you approach the corner of Pine and Magnolia Avenue, look for a place to put your car for a minute, or—if you are on foot—walk to the corner of Pine and Magnolia. At 37-39 South Magnolia Avenue—the northeast corner of Pine and Magnolia—is one of downtown's prettiest historic buildings: the **Rogers Building (#11)**. It was built between 1886 and 1887 for Gordon Rogers, who had come to Orlando from England in 1883. He operated a business downstairs, and upstairs he installed the English Club—designed as a place of refuge for settlers from England. The south and west sides of the building have the original pressed tin panels imported from the United Kingdom. There are stories about this building being haunted—but with or without ghosts, the lovely restoration of the Rogers

Photo by Gene Randall

Building does make the spirit (or spirits as the case may be) soar.

Now continue on Pine to Rosalind Avenue, turn left on Rosalind and left again on the next street, Central Boulevard. On your right-hand side as you drive on Central, you'll find the **Orange County Public Library (#12)**. There are a few temporary parking spots in front of it. If you are in your car, pull into one of them for a minute. This has been the site of Orlando's library for more than 80 years. In 1921, Col. Charles Lewis Albertson donated his book collection to the city, on the condition that the city build a public library. It opened here in 1923. The present building dates to 1966—a time during which architects were experimenting with designs like the one used here. Not everybody likes this building, but few people find themselves without an opinion on the merits of its design. I always think it looks like it needs a good scrubbing. There is a public parking garage across the street if you would like to leave your car and continue on foot.

Continue going west on Central, and just past the intersection of Central and Magnolia, look to your right and you'll see Orlando's 1927 **Orange County Courthouse (#13)**, now home to the **Orange County Regional History Center**. (Once again, if you are driving, you can pull briefly to your right and sit for a minute if you don't park and get out.) Kudos to the city and county for preserving this historic building. In **Heritage Square (#14)**—the park out in front of the History Center—there used to be a useful but unattractive courthouse annex, which was torn down. The square is now used for the **Orlando Farmers Market**, held every Saturday morning. See if you can

Bunk Baxter?

spot the sculpture honoring Bunk Baxter, a somewhat mythical Orlando character from the city's past, known for his prowess at wrestling gators. On the right side of the street, between Court Avenue and Orange at 17-19 East Central, is a beautiful old red brick building called the **Christ Building (#15)**. Dr. C. D. Christ had it built between 1903 and 1910 for a private sanitarium and hospital. He was a surgeon and one of the founders of Orange Memorial Hospital, now Orlando Regional Medical Center. The building now carries a pretty brass plaque detailing its interesting history.

Turn left onto South Orange Avenue and walk or drive to **Orlando City Hall (#16)**, a $32 million structure opened in June 1991. It is on the southwest corner of Orange and South Street. There is parking out front. As mentioned before, the previous city hall was blown up (imploded, actually), a scene that appears at the beginning of *Lethal Weapon 3*. This building sat adjacent to the old structure during the implosion, and not even a memo stirred upon its new desks as the old city hall crashed to the ground.

Inside city hall, on the ground floor, is the **Terrace Gallery**, a free art exhibit space. Upstairs on the third floor is the **Mayor's Gallery**, another free gallery. If you feel

City Hall. Photo by Gene Randall.

like taking a break, sit down in the one of the rocking chairs on city hall's "front porch." Not only are they comfortable, but they also help give this imposing structure a welcoming look.

Once back on foot or in your car, head down Orange one more block to Anderson Street and turn left. (This maneuver requires you to cross three lanes of traffic, so look for an opening and move in with gusto.) Turn left again at Rosalind. We are now headed for the prettiest part of this tour: the area surrounding **Lake Eola**. At Central turn right. On your left, Lake Eola will come into view. Look for the **Sperry Fountain (#17)**, dedicated in 1914, on the edge of the lake. It is named for E. F. Sperry the owner of the South Foundry and Machine Works who donated some land to the city and also paid for the fountain.

If you see a place to park adjacent to 300 Central (on either side of the street), take it and walk toward the lake. You'll find two plaques there. The first, called the **Marks Plaque (#18)** honors Matthew Marks, who served as mayor from 1889 to 1890 and who started a program of tree planting in Orlando. Across the walkway from the Marks Plaque is a plaque honoring the **Centennial Fountain (#19)**,

Fountain at Lake Eola. Orlando, Fla.

Sperry Fountain in a vintage postcard from the collection of Russell V. Hughes.

ORLANDO, FLORIDA, THE CITY BEAUTIFUL.   O-52

THE SKY-LINE FROM ACROSS LAKE EOLA.   105198

which is the dramatic feature at the center of Lake Eola. The fountain was formally dedicated on October 5, 1957, and in 1966, its name was changed to the **Linton E. Allen Fountain** to honor the businessman who led the campaign to have it built. I have a friend who calls this fountain "the big Jell-O mold." You have to admit, there is an aptness to this description.

Continue east on Central to Eola Drive, turn left on Eola and then right into the **Thornton Park Central** parking garage **(#20)**—assuming you haven't been able to find parking on the street, which is hard to come by here adjacent to Lake Eola. Parking in the garage will leave you free to explore the lakeside on foot while your car stays cool. Walk back to Lake Eola, and head for the large live oak with the blue tables underneath. Angle right, toward the wooden walkway above the lake and then look to your left (to the west). First you'll see the **Walt Disney Amphitheater (#21)** in the distance. This went up in 1989 and is the spring home of the **Orlando-UCF Shakespeare Theater**, which produces an annual repertory of the Bard's plays. It is the fourth such structure on the lake. The previous bandshells/stages went up in 1918, 1924, and 1962 at several spots around the lake.

On the wooden walkway, you'll see a number of bronze busts honoring distinguished leaders from around the world. One of them is the **Bolivar Monument (#22)**, which was presented to the City of Orlando in 1996 by the president of the Republic of Venezuela. If you keep walking east on the sidewalk surrounding Lake Eola, you'll reach the **Reeves Monument (#23)**, which sits under a tree. In

1939, this was dedicated by the students of Cherokee Junior High School to the memory of Orlando Reeves—a man we are not even sure existed, but after whom some believe the City of Orlando was named. He was supposed to have been a soldier killed here in battle with the Indians in 1835. No one is certain if that story is true, but the legend persists.

You'll find a touching plaque nearby. It is the **World War I Monument (#24)**, dedicated in 1924 by the Daughters of the American Revolution " … to the Orlando boys" who died in " … the World War." The reference to "boys" is so sadly accurate; and the article "the" before the words "World War" recalls a time when more than one World War was unimaginable.

The Civil War Memorial (#25) This monument has had a bit of a rough time. It went up in 1911 in the middle of the intersection of Magnolia and Central, which is just where it should have remained. But in 1917 Americans thought it was wonderful to "modernize" their cities and roads to accommodate the automobile, so the poor fellow was moved to Lake Eola's park. He originally faced north, to symbolize the men who marched that direction off to war. Now he faces west, which carries no symbolism whatsoever. Then, in 1964, some knuckleheads broke off the rifle and scattered the bits around. Albin Polasek, the Czech sculptor who lived in Winter Park at the time, was nice enough to repair the statue at no charge. Perhaps this monument is controversial in modern times because it honors the Confederate soldier. The

View of Orange County Court House, Soldiers' Monument, Elks Club and San Juan Hotel, Orlando, Fla.

The Civil War Memorial used to sit in the intersection of Magnolia and Central. It is seen here in a vintage postcard from the collection of Russell V. Hughes.

fact is, Florida was a member of the CSA, and sad to say, all the soldiers who fought in the Civil War—still the bloodiest war in U.S. history—were Americans.

The Chinese Garden (#26) This was presented to the City of Orlando, by the city of Taipei, Republic of China. The large black marble slab is from the mountains of Hua-Lien County.

Musselwhite Monument (#27) Jacob Summerlin is known as the man who deeded Lake Eola to the city. But J. P. Musselwhite had a part in the park too. In the 1890s, he bought the land between Lake Eola and Summerlin Avenue and donated it to the city to complete the park.

Battle of the Bulge Monument (#28) (This is on the northeast side of the lake.) D-Day was long past and the Allies were winning the war when snowy weather bogged down their advance across France in December 1944. The Battle of the Bulge involved some of the toughest fighting of World War II. This monument, dedicated in 1999, honors the U.S. servicemen who fought in that battle.

Now that you've toured the lake, you can walk back to Washington, and take Washington east to Summerlin. Here, you'll find yourself in the heart of **Thornton Park**, one of Orlando's newest, newly redone, older districts. You've left your car in the Thornton Park Central parking garage, right? Why not take some time to stroll around this wonderful gentrified neighborhood, full of shops, restaurants, and older homes. Entrepreneur Phil Rampy was behind much of this area's resurgence. He built

UrbanThink Bookstore is a great Thornton Park hangout.

a restaurant, spa, and hotel here and suddenly, Thornton Park was hip. **UrbanThink Bookstore**, on Central, is a local gathering place for people fond of books and wine. Enjoy yourself in this pretty district before ending your stroll through Orlando history.

Local historian Steve Rajtar did all the groundwork for this tour, which is an amalgam—with his kind permission—of two of the Historical Trails he has devised for downtown Orlando. For more on his Florida walking tours, contact Steve at rajtar@aol.com and he will direct you to his Central Florida Historical Trails site on the Web.

College Park
Driving or Biking Tour

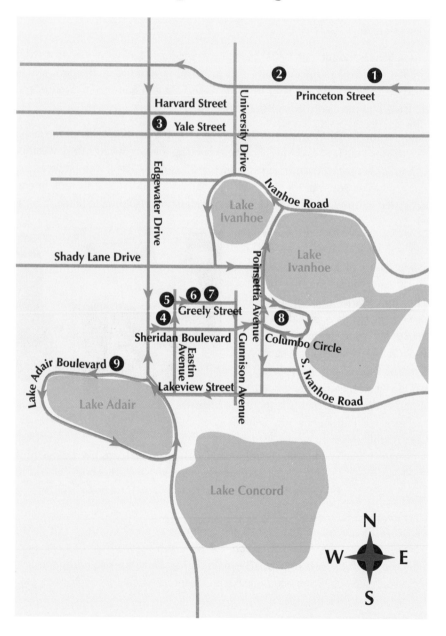

College Park's Lake Adair.

A Unique Orlando Neighborhood
CHARMING COLLEGE PARK

C ollege Park is one of the most distinctive neighborhoods within the Orlando city limits. Because it includes three nice-sized lakes, it has always been a desirable place, both for agriculture and for homes. After the Civil War, several hearty pioneers homesteaded or bought property for citrus groves near Lakes Adair and Ivanhoe. In 1885, a fellow named George Russell bought the land around Lake Ivanhoe for an amusement park. The railroad was completed to Central Florida about then, and tourists were coming for the first time. Russell built what was—in a way—Orlando's first theme park.

Just after World War I, developers Cooper and Atha bought Russell's amusement park and subdivided it for building lots. This was another boom time for Orlando. In 1923, entrepreneur Carl Dann bought a hog farm in College Park, subdivided the lots, built a golf course in the middle that he called Dubsdread, and sold the lots at a tidy profit. He finished the project just in time. By 1927, the Florida boom had gone bust, and in 1929, the bust turned into the Great Depression.

Since there is no college in College Park, where did the name come from? The simple answer is, it came from the fertile imaginations of developers. Naming streets after famous colleges was considered a very classy thing to do in the 1920s, and that's when a lot of College Park was developed. You'll notice Yale, Dartmouth, Amherst, Harvard, Cornell, and DePauw among the many college names used on College Park streets. Since Carl Dann built many of his houses beside a golf course, his streets have golf-y names like Par and Greens. Street names like Guernsey reflect the fact that there was a large dairy in College Park for many years.

This neighborhood tour of College Park is five miles and designed for you to complete in your car or on your bicycle. Either way, it won't take you much more than an hour—probably less.

Begin by taking Exit 85 (Princeton Street) off I-4 and turning left (west) onto Princeton. There are a couple of things to look for on the right as you drive toward Edgewater. At **19 West Princeton (#1)**, you'll see an old pink farmhouse with a white picket fence out in front. This home dates from the 1880s when much of the property in this neighborhood was owned by pioneer James Wilcox. Farther up on your right you'll see **Princeton Elementary School (#2)**, opened in 1927. Carl Dann III (grandson of the developer) says that during World War II, housing was so tight that his family had to rent rooms to pilots training at the air base. All of them, says Dann, fell in love with his beautiful mother. "Oh my dear," she used to tell them, "I'm much too old for you. You see I have a son at *Princeton*." She was referring to Princeton Elementary.

The old Dixie Highway is now Edgewater Drive, and you can still use it as route between Orlando and Apopka. Postcard from the Florida State Archives.

Peter Schreyer, Executive Director of Crealdé School of Art, put this picture of the College Park Publix on a poster seen all over Europe. Photo by Peter Schreyer.

When you reach Edgewater Drive, turn left. Travel about a block, until you cross Harvard, and look to your left. You'll see the most amazing Publix Supermarket at **2015 Edgewater (#3)**. Pull into the parking lot if you want to really appreciate the place. The College Park Neighborhood Association published a tour a few years ago which says that this store dates from 1950, and the design does suggest that period. Lee Brunson at Publix says this store opened in 1967 and though I questioned him on that date he was very firm. Anyway, the store was completely re-done in 1998, but this wonderful design was spared.

Turn left (south) onto Edgewater, and look for Sheridan Street, where you will turn left. Travel one block to Eastin Avenue and turn left again. At **1318** and **1322 Eastin (#4 & #5)**, you'll see two of the first homes built in this section of College Park, called Adair Park. Designer Sam Stoltz was behind these two designs. Stoltz called the style of 1318 Eastin "Spanish Orlando" and lived there himself for a while in 1926-1927. He was known for the unusual details he designed into each house.

Turn right onto Greely Street. As you drive down Greely, look for **610 Greely**, and **533 Greely (#6 & #7)**. Sam Stoltz designed all or parts of these homes for contractor E. M. Carey. Most of the decorative touches were done by Stoltz himself, and all are as quirky and interesting as he was. Continue on Greely to Gunnison

College Park in a vintage postcard from the collection of Russell V. Hughes.

Avenue (where you can only turn right), and then turn left onto Sheridan. If you make a gentle left down the hill, you'll be on Poinsettia Avenue, and it will take you along the shore of Lake Ivanhoe. Here, you'll see some lovely homes on your left and the lake on your right. Cross the little bridge, and when you reach the stop sign at Ivanhoe Boulevard, turn left and follow the road around this small inlet in the lake. The homes on your right are gorgeous—and that's an understatement. West Ivanhoe Boulevard will end at Shady Lane. Turn left on Shady Lane, and then turn right when you again reach Poinsettia.

Follow Poinsettia until you see South Ivanhoe and turn left. On your right, not far up the road, at **1338 Ivanhoe (#8)**, is a home built in 1936. The architect was Maurice Kressly of Orlando, who was known for the romantic style of his designs. The contractor was Thomas F. Kenney, who built the house for himself and his family. The College Park Neighborhood Association spoke with Kenney's daughter, Colleen Gentry, a decade ago, and she said the bricks used in the house are street bricks from a defunct subdivision off Lake Killarney. The style of the home is called Tudor Revival. It is difficult to see the garage because of the foliage, but at the top of the garage is a birdhouse built into the gable. This section of College Park is called Ivanhoe Park, platted in 1919.

As you move on, turn right on Columbo, left on Poinsettia, right on Lakeview, and right on Edgewater. Quickly move into the left-hand lane so you can turn left onto **Lake Adair Boulevard (#9)**. I don't have any specific addresses for you to look for here: the homes are so beautiful and posh that I thought you might just enjoy the view. Don't you wonder how people handle the maintenance on homes this large? I can't even get anybody to come out and fix the motor on my electric garage door opener.

There is an easy place to turn around at Westmoreland, where there is a round-about—assuming you've done enough gaping and gasping at the houses. Head back to Edgewater and turn left. Look for West Yale Street and turn right. This puts you in the original College Park subdivision laid out in 1925 by CABCO—Cooper, Atha, Barr Real Estate Company. Look for **520 West Yale (#10)**, a small, simple house, typical of those built for the middle class in 1938-1939. It has casement windows, Colonial detailing, and a gable roof. It probably sold to its original buyer for just a few thousand dollars.

Our brief tour of College Park is complete. You can follow Yale to University Drive, turn left and then right again on Princeton if you are ready to move on. Or you can return to Edgewater, park in one of the metered spaces, and stroll through the College Park business district, enjoying the interesting shops and small restaurants. This unique shopping district helps make College Park the community it is, as it moves into the 21st century, with its 20th-century charm.

> *This tour is a modified version of one produced by the College Park Neighborhood Association Historical Committee in 1992. I thank the association for allowing me to steal shamelessly from their research.*

A BEAUTY SPOT, ORLANDO, FLORIDA

ECO-TOURING

FLORIDA BIRDS

BLUE HERON
(Ardea Herodias)

SNOWY HERON
(Egretta Candidissima)

WHOOPING CRANE
(Grus Americana)

WOOD IBIS
(Tantalus Loculator)

© CURT TEICH & CO., INC.

9A

Florida Hibiscus

ECO-TOURING

Whither Do They Wander?

AS NATIVE TO FLORIDA
AS A PINK FLAMINGO

Y ou may imagine there are flamingos everywhere you go in Florida. There are certainly enough of them on Florida postcards to make you think so. There are also a who lot of Florida motels, hotels, gardens, and attractions with "flamingo" in the name. However, there are not now, and very likely never were, native flamingos in Florida. Early observers of the Greater Flamingo, also known as *Phoenicopterus ruber*, were able to spot them occasionally in the Florida Keys. Fishermen told the naturalist John James Audubon (1785-1851) that there were some flamingo nests in the Keys, but he was never able to prove that. He believed the flamingos that were seen from time to time on the very tip of South Florida were there in search of food and returned to their homes father south when they wrapped up their fishing expeditions. The Greater Flamingos' prime nesting places are the Caribbean and the area between Mexico's Yucatan and the northern tip of South America.

Edward Bok tried to introduce them into Historic Bok Sanctuary in Lake Wales, believing they had once been native. But though he tried Greater Flamingos, Chilean Flamingos, and African Flamingos, none of them took to Central Florida. Feeding them the shrimp that is an essential part of their diet (that's

The flamingos looked great at Bok Towers, but they didn't last.
Vintage postcard from the Florida State Archives.

what makes them pink) was expensive during World War II. In 1944 the last one died, and it wasn't replaced.

The name of the bird comes from the Spanish word *flamenco*, which can mean "flame-like" or, in another sense, "like a gypsy." Perhaps its brightly colored feathers inspired the early Spanish explorers to make this association: perhaps the birds' inclination to roam was the inspiration. In any case, if you see a flamingo in Central Florida today, it either is very lost, is part of a tourist attraction, or is AWOL from one—a sort of hot pink jailbird.

This 1965 photo was snapped by the late Florida State Archivist Dorothy Dodd in a stream near Saint Marks in the Florida panhandle. It appears to discredit my story that flamingos don't live in Florida, but—especially this far north—it is almost certainly an escapee from a tourist attraction or zoo. It looks very lovely fishing there though, doesn't it? Photo courtesy of the Florida State Archives.

WHERE EAGLES PAIR

A s you drive, walk, or bike around Central Florida, you might ask someone in your group to keep watch on the skies above you. Florida is home to more than 2,000 American Bald Eagles—more eagles than in any other state in the Union except Alaska. Central Florida is the primary residence of more than one-third of those eagles. The county with the state's highest eagle population (119 pairs in a recent census) is Osceola County, just south of Orlando. Polk County, adjacent to Osceola, is second in the state, with 118 pairs. Add to this

© *Hammond World Atlas Corp.*

the eagle pairs in Lake County (70), Brevard County (42), and Orange County (32), and you'll find there are at least 381 pairs, or 762 eagles, to spot while you visit Central Florida. Look for very large nests in the tops of cypress and slash pine trees. Eagles return to the same nests year after year, and their annual repairs add to the nests' size. The American Bald Eagle is one of the largest birds on the North American continent, with a 7-to-8-foot wingspan. If you are lucky enough to see one gliding in the thermals above you, it will be difficult to mistake it for any other bird. Much of the Walt Disney World Resort is in Osceola County, and the wide-open spaces on the resort's property and its many bodies of water make it prime eagle-watching territory.

Between January and April, the Florida State Audubon Society and the Orlando Sentinel monitor an eagle's nest somewhere in Central Florida via a live video camera. You can access the video on the Web and watch a fledgling hatch and grow. Log on to www.orlandosentinel.com/news/orl-eaglewatch.special. The annual eagle census is conducted by the Florida State Fish and Wildlife Conservation Commission with the assistance of Audubon Society EagleWatch volunteers. Call **407-644-0190** for more information.

Audubon Center
FOR THE BIRDS

© Hammond World Atlas Corp.

I t is always an experience to see a bird of prey, such as an eagle, hawk, or owl, in the wild. But not everyone gets the opportunity to do that. One alternative is to visit the Audubon of Florida's Center for Birds of Prey in Maitland, just a few miles north of downtown Orlando. Since the center opened in 1979, it has received more than 10,000 injured birds, about 8,000 of which have been eagles, hawks, owls, falcons, kites, and vultures—called birds of prey, or raptors. The Audubon Society is able to rehabilitate and release something like 40 percent of these injured birds back into the wild. Some of the birds that live and yet are not able to survive in the wild are given to zoos and educational facilities across the country. Others remain at the center and are used to enlighten people about the 26 different species of raptors that live in Florida. This is what makes the center worth a visit. In its outdoor aviaries on the shores of Lake Sybelia, the Audubon Society hosts everything from a bald eagle couple—Prairie and T.J.—to a tiny Burrowing Owl—so small, and so much like the color of a tree—it is tough to spot as it snoozes through the daylight hours. On a recent visit, I saw a Barn Owl couple asleep at the top of a ladder, and a Barred Owl resting with its head apparently turned all the way around backwards—an Exorcist-like trick that is no sweat for an owl. As I stood watching the falcons, ospreys, and hawks, a Great Blue Heron floated unhindered across the sky and landed nearby at the edge of the lake.

The Audubon of Florida's Center for Birds of Prey is at 1101 Audubon Way, Maitland, Florida 32751. Open Tuesday-Sunday, 10:00 a.m. to 4:00 p.m. Small admission donation. Take Exit 88 off I-4, going east (toward Winter Park). Just off the exit, turn left (north) onto Wymore Road. Take Wymore to Kennedy Boulevard and turn right (east) onto Kennedy. Take Kennedy to East Avenue and turn left. Turn left again onto Audubon Way. **407-644-0190.** www.audubonofflorida.org.

Florida's Endangered Treasure
THE MANATEE

Florida is one of just three places remaining in the world where you can see the gentle marine mammal called the manatee. It is the only marine mammal that is an herbivore—that means it grazes on green things, like a cow. And, though it is sometimes called a sea cow, its closest relative is actually the elephant. Like the elephant it is one of the largest creatures in its habitat: the average adult manatee is 10 feet long (2.5 to 4.5 m) and weighs about 1,000 pounds (200 to 600 kg). Think about that for a minute. This is a *very* large animal to come across in a river.

© Hammond World Atlas Corp.
This cute little fellow must be a baby manatee, as most of the adults are about the size of a large refrigerator.

The creature we call the Florida manatee is really a subspecies of the West Indian Manatee or *Trichechus manatus*. It is one of three species of related seagoing mammals of the order *Sirenia*. The name *Sirenia* harks back to stories told by early sailors who mistook the manatee for the "sirens" of Greek legend—mermaids who lured ships onto the rocks. As it turns out, manatees are much too friendly to do any such evil luring, and the animals don't look anything like beautiful mermaids. Clearly, sailors who were away from women for years at a time on those tiny sailing ships developed vivid imaginations.

The manatee is so large it has no natural enemies, and its brain isn't programmed to fear. Consequently, these animals are curious and very friendly toward land-based mammals like you and me. You aren't supposed to swim with them and bother them, as they are protected from harassment by

Boaters can't always see manatees and collisions occur.

both federal and state law, but people who accidentally come upon manatees in Florida rivers and streams report that they seem to love swimming near humans and will roll over on their backs like cats or dogs (though considerably larger) and practically purr if they get a petting or a back scratch.

> Related manatees can be found in the Amazon basin (*Trichechus inunguis*) and in West Africa (*Trichechus senegalensis*). There is a related mammal called the dugong that lives in the Red Sea, the Indian Ocean, and along the coast of Australia, and these too are protected because of their dwindling numbers.

Unfortunately, some humans have been unfriendly in return. A cousin of the manatee, the Stellar's Sea Cow was hunted to extinction in the 18th century. The Florida manatee is presently facing many challenges from humans: watercraft propellers and impact injuries are the leading causes of manatee deaths. Pollution is also a danger. There is much debate in Florida about what can be done to preserve them. The good ecological news is that after a low in the 1970s, their numbers appear to be on the rise.

So when you see a manatee in the wild in Florida you are really seeing a treasure. Though they disperse throughout the coastal areas when the weather is warm, *Trichechus manatus* always gather inland at Florida's warm springs in the winter. You might call them Florida's first, and most reliable snowbirds.

This photo and the photo at left, courtesy of the Florida Fish and Wildlife Conservation Commission.

D.L. 15   BLUE SPRINGS, NEAR DE LAND, FLA.

*If you were being picky, you might notice this vintage postcard goof:
the name of the park is Blue Spring, not Springs.*

MANATEE WINTER SPA

Blue Spring State Park From November through March, one of the best places to see manatees in the wild—within easy driving distance of Orlando—is Blue Spring State Park. The park, which is between Orlando and Daytona Beach, is a sort of winter spa for manatees, and on a cool day it can be home to more than a hundred of them. Park rangers have become familiar with the Blue Spring regulars and have given them nicknames like Flash, Deep Dent, No Tail, and Nick, to reflect the animals' various motorboat injuries. In Blue Spring the manatees are protected from boats, canoes, and swimmers, and here they rest after chowing down on sea grass and aquatic plants in the nearby St. Johns River. They nurse their young, loll about, and mostly they sleep. The park has a boardwalk adjacent to the spring, from which you can watch the animals without bothering them. I think the best place to see them is down at the end of the boardwalk near the swimming dock. There, you can get down closest to the water, and the manatees will often swim right up to check you out. Who knows? Maybe one of the things the manatees like about Blue Spring is that it's a great place to come to watch the people.

*To reach Blue Spring State Park take Exit 54 off I-4. Go south on Route 17-92 to Orange City—about 2.5 miles. Turn right onto West French Avenue to 2100 West French Avenue, Orange City. The park is open from 8:00 a.m. until sunset 365 days a year. Call **386-775-3663** for more information, or log on to: www.dep.state.fl.us/parks/district3/bluespring/index.asp*

SeaWorld's Rescue Program
MANATEE R AND R

Y ou can't always find a manatee in the wild in Florida. In the summer, when the coastal waters are warm, manatees disperse around Florida's coast, visiting the state's coastal rivers, bays, and estuaries. Some venture north to the Carolinas or west to Louisiana or Texas. If you come to Central Florida in the summer, a sure place to see manatees is SeaWorld, where SeaWorld's animal care staff operates a full-time manatee rescue program. Orphaned calves are brought to SeaWorld, along with injured adults. With care, many of them can be released back into the wild after their rehabilitation. The Florida Fish and Wildlife Conservation Commission works with programs like the one at SeaWorld to help preserve this marine mammal. The work is paying off. The manatee count in Florida in 1991 was 1,465. Ten years later, the number had risen to more than 3,000. Florida's analysis shows that if present conditions continue, the manatee will not be extinct in 100 years, as some feared a decade ago. SeaWorld's manatee exhibit is called *Manatees: The Last Generation?* As efforts continue, many in Florida hope that title is already out of date.

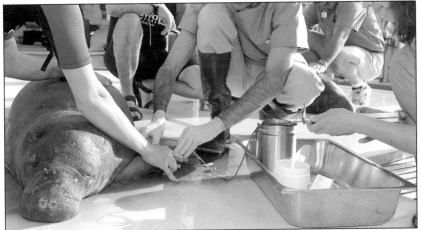

©2003 SeaWorld of Florida

All of the manatees at SeaWorld have been rescued from the wild, and those nursed back to health are returned to the wild as well.

To reach SeaWorld Adventure Park follow directions previously indicated in the section on SeaWorld. To visit the manatee exhibit you must buy a one-day ticket to the park. Phone **407-351-3600** or log on to www.seaworld.com.

Coreopsis is the Florida state wildflower. Photo by Phil Esbach.

WATCHING FOR WILDFLOWERS

The Florida state wildflower is the Coreopsis, commonly called Tickseed because the fruit of the plant looks a bit like a bug. There are at least 13 Coreopsis species you can see in Florida, and two of those aren't seen anywhere else. The *Coreopsis floridana* and the *Coreopsis leavenworthii* are Florida exclusive. All the species have yellow flowers except one: the Coreopsis nudata, also known as swamp tickseed, has pink flowers just to be different. Most of the Coreopsis plants in Florida are truly wildflowers—meaning they are native and uncultivated. But in recent years, the Florida Department of Transportation has been sowing Coreopsis seeds along the shoulders of Florida highways including *Coreopsis lanceolata, Coreopsis tinctoria, Coreopsis basalis,* and *Coreopsis leavenworthii.*

This is a great state wildflower, since different species bloom at various times of the year, and a month rarely goes by when a Coreopsis isn't blooming somewhere in Florida. So, if you're stuck in traffic on your visit to Central Florida (not that you will be) why not play a game with your fellow strandees? See which of you can spot a clump of roadside Coreopsis first. If you can distinguish among the species, you're a better botanist than I am. The University of Florida has a pamphlet that will help. It is called "A Guide to Identifying and Enjoying Florida's State Wildflower." Contact the university's Institute of Food and Agricultural Sciences if you would like to request one.

Write North Florida Research and Education Center, 155 Research Road, Quincy, Florida 32351 for the pamphlet. Or log on to www.ifas.ufl.edu. My thanks to Keep Winter Park Beautiful for the information on Florida's state wildflower.

MORE FLOWERS OF WILD LA FLORIDA

C entral Florida is home to at least 32 species of wildflowers and plants that are either threatened or endangered. Learning to identify them is a means of preserving them. If you see them in the wild, take the action you would take on a modern African safari: take nothing away but pictures. Here are a few examples of endangered Florida beauty, all photographed by the late Florida Archivist Dorothy Dodd.

Snowy Orchid

Its common name is the Bog Torch, and it is one of Florida's true wild orchids. It blooms from June through September during the state's hottest, dampest months and can be found, if you are lucky, along the St. Johns River. But you have to look hard: it is only about 3 inches tall.

Yellow Fringed Orchid

The Yellow Fringed Orchid has quite a bit of orange in it, and it crosses easily with the orange variety if the two plants grow near one another. It flowers from July to September in meadows and open woods. The plant is tiny: only about 1 inch to 2 1/2 inches high.

Rose Pogonia

Also called Snake Mouth. They say the fragrance of the rose-pink flowers is like the scent of raspberry. Most likely to be found along the coast.

Photos by Dorothy Dodd

Rainlily

This is a flower native Floridians call the Easter Lily because it blooms near Easter time. It is an herb with a sweet scent, with each plant—8 inches to 12 inches long—holding just one flower.

Politically Incorrect
HANDBAGS WITH FEET

There are about a million alligators in the state of Florida, or about one gator for every 17 people. I see that as an awful lot of handbags, belts, and shoes—forgive me, please—I'm just a nut for accessories. The alligator (*Alligator mississippiensis*) was categorized as endangered under the 1973 Endangered Species Act, but by 1977, this resilient reptile had rebounded so far that its status was downgraded to threatened. It isn't even threatened today, but it is still protected since an alligator looks very much like a cayman and a crocodile, and the government controls trade in those creatures, which are endangered. So, Florida limits what is known, ahem, as the alligator *harvest*, and limits the number of people in the state allowed to raise gators on farms to just 30. Consequently, these ugly predators pretty much have the run of Florida. They live in water hazards on golf courses, (why do you think they call them "hazards?"), lagoons, sloughs, rivers, streams, and just about every other wet place in Florida, except swimming pools, and that's probably coming next. When I was a reporter, we once heard a call on the police radio that a gator had been found under a car at one of Orlando's most prominent automobile dealerships. Alligator attacks on humans are rare, but 13 people have been killed in Florida in the last 50 years by alligators, and more than half of those fatal attacks have come just since 1993. I once fell out of a canoe into a local lake. When I remembered they called the place Alligator Cove, I set a new speed record for getting back into a canoe from the water without using a dock. Ever since then I've always liked my gators best with a nice shoulder strap and a suede lining.

From the look in this gator's eye, I can see he knows he's protected. Ha!

Even More Politically Incorrect
GATOR GASTRONOMY

ince there are 30 legal alligator farms in the State of Florida, I thought perhaps you might like to contribute to Florida's economy by putting a little gator on your dinner table. Don't feel bad for the poor creatures: we've got a million of 'em.

One of my neighbors who has lived in Central Florida for a long time took this picture in 1938 of a gator in the driveway of what is now my home! Photo by Peggy Strong.

Alligator Stew
Temperature: medium heat   Cooking time: 1 hour

1/2 cup vegetable oil
1 quart cut-up alligator meat
1/2 cup chopped onion
1/2 cup chopped bell pepper
1/2 cup chopped celery

2 tablespoons minced parsley
1 10-ounce can tomatoes with green chilies
salt and pepper
1 cup cooked rice

Put vegetable oil and alligator meat in heavy 4-quart cooking pot. Add chopped vegetables, parsley, and tomatoes. Season with salt and pepper. Cover pot and cook over medium heat for one hour. Serve over hot cooked rice.

Alligator Meatballs
Temperature: high   Preparation time: 1 hour

1 pound alligator meat, chopped
1 egg
1 tablespoon onion, chopped fine
2 tablespoons celery, chopped fine
1 tablespoon parsley, chopped fine
2 tablespoons shallots, chopped fine

2 teaspoons lemon pepper
1/2 teaspoon salt
1/4 cup bread crumbs
flour
1 cup cooking oil

Mix all ingredients; form into 1-inch balls. Allow to sit for 1 hour. Dredge with flour and fry until brown. Serve hot.

The above recipes come to us from the Louisiana Seafood Board, where they clearly have the right idea about what to do with a gator. www.LouisianaSeafood.com.

MORE FLORA AND FAUNA IN THE SUBTROPICS

American Egret There are four different species of egrets in Florida from the Great to the Snowy to the Reddish to the Cattle Egret, all members of the Heron family. The egret is an ecological success story: hunted almost to extinction at the turn of the century for their feathers, which were used to adorn women's hats, they are now fully recovered—though still protected. There was rejoicing in the North when these beautiful birds began returning in the summer months.

Great Blue Heron At 4 feet in length, when one of these birds takes to the air, it looks like a small plane. They love to fish, and since Florida has 7,700 lakes, they find excellent fishing available. Most common in Central Florida from November through April, they choose to spend the summer in cooler climes.

The **Eastern Brown Pelican** is a year-round resident of the Florida coast. If you've seen them fish, you'll never forget it: they zoom along just above the ocean, climb 20 or 30 feet in the air, and then dive directly into the water. Splash! They emerge carrying a fish. The White Pelican is found inland in Florida, and isn't nearly as spectacular a fisherbird.

This is the tree you imagine should be in Florida, and it is a native: the **Coconut Palm**. Called by the Spanish *coco*—which literally means bogeyman—they arrive as coconuts on sandy beaches, where they sprout roots and grow into trees. They don't, however, migrate inland on their own. Most coconut palms you see inland from the coast arrived there on trucks.

Live Oak This is the native oak of Florida and the Gulf States. The Timucuan Indians used its acorns for food, and the Spanish used it for ship building. It is the oak of Orlando's Big Tree Park, and it gives Spanish Moss a place to be on permanent display.

Paintings by Walter Ferguson © Hammond World Atlas Corp.

Ever wonder what that sound is near sunset in the summer in Orlando? It is the sound of the **Cicada** (*Magicicada septendecim*). The newly hatched adults emerge after 13 years in the ground, leave their nymphal shell behind, climb a tree, and then vibrate the membranes of their thoraxes to produce that whirring sound. They live just long enough to mate and begin the 13-year cycle all over again.

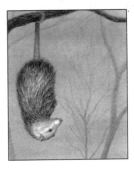

The **Opossum** is very common in Florida, and throughout the southern states. The local paper recently reported on a baby that had taken up residence—uninvited—in a Central Florida home. Rufus, as he was dubbed, sneaked around and ate the family dog's food and went on night raids of their pantry. Did we say possums love to scavenge? When confronted, this small mammal with the opposable thumbs, falls to the ground and appears to be dead. But it's not: it is just "playing possum."

Alligator A recent notice from the Winter Park Lakes Division urges citizens of Central Florida to " … never leave dogs or children unattended around shorelines." Guess why? If you do see a nuisance gator, you are urged to call the Florida Fish and Wildlife Commission, at **352-732-1225** for "removal." Those state rangers have all the fun.

Photographer David O. Stillings calls this photo "Light Up Orlando."
Stillings is also known as the Lightning Stalker.

WILD WEATHER

Lightning   Central Florida weather is filled with drama. When the sun shines, it really shines. When it storms: look out! In fact, the National Weather Service has dubbed Central Florida "lightning alley." More people are struck by lightning in Central Florida, and more people are killed by it, than in any other spot in North America. Central Florida is the lightning capital of the United States.

Most of the lightning storms take place between May and October and between the hours of noon and midnight. People in fishing boats and swimming pools or on golf courses and tennis courts are especially vulnerable; and these are the things people come to Orlando to do. The odds of someone in the United States being hit by lightning are 1 in 600,000. But that's the average and includes states where there is almost no lightning at all: assume the odds are shorter in Central Florida. Put another way, you are much more likely to be hit by a bolt of lightning in Orlando than you are to win the lottery.

The weather service suggests people follow the "30/30 rule," and here is what they mean by that: if you see lightning and can count to 30 (or less) between the lightning and the thunder—between the "flash" and the "crash"—it is time to come in from the storm. Wait 30 minutes after you hear the last clap of thunder before you go back outside. This rule applies because lightning can occur on both the leading and trailing edges of a storm, and it can strike from a seemingly clear sky—hence the term "a bolt from the blue," which is a very real phenomenon.

I once interviewed a young man who had been riding his motorcycle from Daytona Beach to Orlando, with his girlfriend on the seat behind him, when a thunderstorm erupted. The rain was heavy but they were almost home, and there wasn't anyplace safe to pull over in any case. Suddenly, a bolt of lightning struck. It blew out all the bike's fuses and knocked the man cold. The young woman had the presence of mind to steer the cycle to the edge of the road, set it down as carefully as she could, and flag down a passing motorist, who called an ambulance. She was unhurt. The man wasn't so lucky. The lightning bolt appeared to have gone in through his helmet and out his right big toe. It seared a black

"E-ticket at Eola." Another spectacular photo from the Lightning Stalker.

"Riders On the Storm," may be the most amazing photo taken by David O. Stillings.

melted patch on the helmet and blew a gold chain off his neck and onto the pavement. But it must not have been a direct hit because he lived to tell about it. He couldn't open his eyes for a couple of days, but he came out of it OK—or at least as OK as one could after having been struck by lighting.

I mention the fact that more than 1,200 people are hit by lightning each year in Florida, not to frighten you but to remind residents and visitors alike of the overwhelming power of nature—and to suggest that everyone in Central Florida have a plan, to avoid becoming a statistic. Things aren't nearly as bad as they could be: the weather in the African nation of Rwanda makes Central Florida's weather look tame by comparison. Rwanda experiences *twice* as much lightning as does Central Florida, and lays claim to the title "lightning capital of the world." This is one contest in which Central Florida does not mind taking second place.

The National Oceanographic and Atmospheric Agency (NOAA) and the National Weather Service operate a Lightning Information Center about 50 miles from Orlando in Melbourne, Florida. You can log on to their Web site at any time of the day or night and see the thunderstorm radar forecast for the region. They also suggest that if you are going to spend a lot of time outdoors in Central Florida in the summer, you buy a small portable radio that receives NOAA forecasts, which are broadcast 24 hours a day. NOAA can be found on the Web at www.srh.noaa.gov. From there, surf to the Lightning Information Center. The University of Florida also maintains a Lightning Research Center. It can be found on the Web at www.light-ning.ece.ufl.edu.

The Lightning Stalker

The Central Florida corridor has so much lightning that it has its very own Lightning Stalker. David O. Stillings has been stalking lightning with his camera since 1976, when someone told him it would be impossible to take pictures of lightning flashes. "I took that as a challenge," says the amateur photographer who has managed to get one or two good lightning shots every year since then. He says he doesn't think he's ever been struck by lightning (I think he would know if he had!), but he has "ended up on the ground" several times, knocked cold by bolts that came too close. All of the photos on these pages are from the Lightning Stalker. If you would like to see more, visit David Stillings' Web site at www.lightningstalker.com. His photo collection is electrifying.

Hurricanes The season for Atlantic hurricanes begins June 1 and ends November 30, and during an average season, 10 storms develop in the Atlantic that are big enough to be given names by the National Hurricane Center. Six of those reach hurricane status, and four don't grow beyond tropical storms. From 1871 through 2001, 1,000 such storms were recorded in the Atlantic; 200 reached Florida, and 75 of those had hurricane force winds—or winds above 73 miles per hour. The

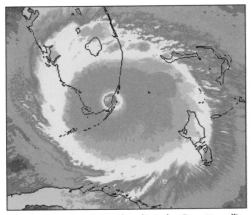

storms generally tend to travel from the Atlantic in a westerly direction, across the Caribbean and Florida and into the Gulf of Mexico, but weather, of course, follows rules of its own, ignoring the artificial borders here on earth.

It has been a long time since Central Florida saw a really big hurricane. One of the largest hit the Orlando area in October 1944 (this was before they began giving the storms

An infrared radar photo taken from the Goes 7 satellite just as the eye of Hurricane Andrew was making landfall in Dade County, Florida August 24, 1992.

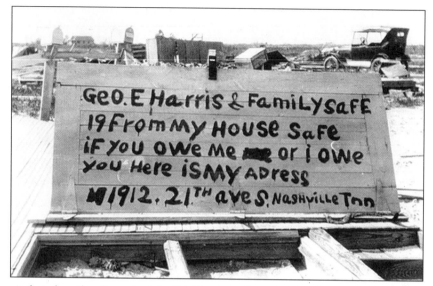

A photo from the aftermath of the 1926 hurricane (hurricanes were not given names back then), which blew through east Central Florida with winds of about 90 mph. This guy gave up and headed for higher ground. Photo courtesy of the Florida State Archives.

names). It had sustained winds of between 158 and 163 mph and tore the roof off the Angebilt Hotel. In the region, 18 people were killed and the damage ran to nearly half a billion dollars.

To some, hurricanes have a special attraction. If you ride one out, you'll witness some pretty amazing things. The drop in barometric pressure as the storm goes over can make your ears pop and your dental fillings ache. Then, after the violence of the first half of the storm, the eye passes over and not a leaf will be stirring. Meteorologist John Williams rode out Hurricane Cleo in South Florida in 1964, according to this account in *Florida Hurricanes and Tropical Storms 1871-2001*:

> The eye passage lasted one hour and twelve minutes at my location …
> I could see the stars in the beautiful sky about me and there was that
> unmistakable stillness and smell that only happens in the eye of a hur-
> ricane. I checked around the house and everything seemed all right …
> [but] now it was time to get back inside the house because the back-
> side of a hurricane comes on like gangbusters.

The Seminole Indians used to say that when the wild oats swayed and fell to the ground, a hurricane was coming in three days. Who knows? If this sort of thing did happen, it may have been caused by the drop in barometric pressure associated with

Lots of locals remember Hurricane Donna in 1960. Donna had peak winds of 180 to 200 mph and brought torrential rains to the state. Her path brought her from Naples, Florida, in a northeasterly direction, across Orlando, and out into the Atlantic at about Ponce Inlet—just south of Daytona Beach. Fifty people were killed, and the flooding damage was extensive.

hurricanes. Today, forecasters have satellite photos and all kinds of electronic equipment to track these storms. If you are in Orlando during hurricane season, check the local weather on television regularly. The Walt Disney World Resort has closed its attractions for a hurricane only once in its entire history. That happened in 1999, and fortunately for Florida the storm took a last-minute turn northward and spared the state. Florida has organized, orderly evacuation plans: it makes sense to stay informed.

You'll probably first hear about any approaching hurricane via word of mouth, but after that, you might want to buy a battery-operated radio if you don't have one on hand. Electrical lines rarely survive hurricane-force winds—unless they are buried underground, which most of Central Florida's lines are not.

903 A PURPLE BOUGAINVILLEA ARBOR
IN THE SUNSHINE STATE, FLORIDA

MODERN CITRUS FRUIT DISPLAY

LICENSED and
BONDED
CHU

GROWERS
PACKERS
SHIPPERS

TR
Daily

SANLANDO SPRINGS, TROPICAL PARK, FLORIDA "THE CITY BEAUTIFUL" O-133

WAY U. S. 17, AT U. S. [9]2, KISSIMMEE, FLA.

BILL

QUALITY P[ ]
SERVI[ ]

FRUIT
SHIPMENTS

CENTRAL
FLORIDA

Skiing is Fun in the Florida Sun

FLAMINGOES AT THE SINGING TOWER
MOUNTAIN LAKE SANCTUARY, FLORIDA—F161

A Tower That Sings

HISTORIC BOK SANCTUARY

There is a beautiful, quiet spot to see flora and fauna just 50 miles south of Orlando, and to absorb a little culture while you are at it. The attraction goes back three quarters of a century, when it was the most famous park in Central Florida. Called "The Mountain Lake Sanctuary and Singing Tower," it was the creation of Edward William Bok (1863-1930), a Dutch immigrant who arrived in the United States in 1870. From the minute he set foot in New York, he began thinking up ways to educate himself and to make money, and he was very good at both. As a teenager, he started his own magazine and press syndicate, and by the time he was 26, he was editor of the most popular magazine of his day: the *Ladies' Home Journal*. The job made him a wealthy man. He also married the publisher's daughter, which didn't hurt his fortunes.

Edward W. Bok

Edward Bok retired in 1919, and he and his wife bought some property in a new development near Lake Wales, Florida, called Mountain Lake. It was set on Iron Mountain, which, at 350 feet above sea level, is the nearest thing Florida has to a mountain. As he built his home, Bok was moved by the beauty of the place, and he began to think about creating a bird sanctuary and nature preserve near his home. Never one just to dream, he bought 20 acres and hired landscape architect Frederick Law Olmsted, Jr.—whose father had designed New York's Central Park—to design the gardens. Nature, it seemed, would have a little assistance. Work began in 1923.

Bok loved the carillon towers of Europe, and he decided to build one in his new attraction at Lake Wales. Though the combination of a bird sanctuary/nature preserve and a carillon tower today sounds a bit quirky, the idea worked for Bok, as so many of his ideas did. The tower was striking and photogenic and—like the theme park "icons" of today—became one of the most recognizable sights in the State of Florida. Bok called it the "singing tower" because of its chiming bells. Completed in 1928, it has provided continuous music to visitors ever since. Beginning in 2003, the tower is being restored, a preservation important to its future and one being completed with both public and private funds.

ANTON BREES PLAYING THE SANCTUARY BELLS AT THE SINGING TOWER

NEAR LAKE WALES, FLA.   11B

For many years, Historic Bok Sanctuary was Central Florida's most famous tourist attraction, so there are many vintage postcards featuring it. These are all from the Florida State Archives.

The park is now 128 acres, bounded by a 4,000-acre nature preserve. It is a good place for bird watching, and for viewing the layout of the gardens promoted by the Olmsteds and other designers of the early 20th century. Most recently, the name has been changed to Historic Bok Sanctuary to reflect its status as a National Historic Landmark.

ENTRANCE TO THE SINGING TOWER AND MOUND WHERE EDWARD W. BOK IS BURIED.

THIS SANCTUARY
WAS CREATED IN 1924 BY EDWARD W. BOK
IT WAS DESIGNED AND EXECUTED BY FREDERICK LAW OLMSTED
ITS PURPOSE IS TO PROVIDE A RETREAT OF REPOSE AND NATURAL
BEAUTY FOR THE HUMAN~A REFUGE FOR THE BIRD~AND A PLACE
FOR THE STUDENT OF SOUTHERN PLANT AND BIRD LIFE

THE SANCTUARY HAS AN AREA OF
FOURTEEN ACRES~ITS PLANTING IS
REPRESENTATIVE OF MUCH OF THE
NATIVE VEGETATION OF FLORIDA~
THE SUMMIT UPON WHICH THIS
ANNOUNCEMENT STANDS IS
ABOUT 324 FEET ABOVE THE SEA

IT IS THE HIGHEST POINT OF LAND
YET MEASURED IN PENINSULAR
FLORIDA~IT IS ALSO THE HIGHEST
LAND WITHIN SIXTY MILES OF THE
ATLANTIC OCEAN AND THE GULF
OF MEXICO BETWEEN WASHINGTON
AND THE RIO GRANDE

FLAMINGOES AT THE MOUNTAIN LAKE SANCTUARY, LAKE WALES, FLORIDA

Historic Bok Sanctuary is open every day from 8:00 a.m. to 6:00 p.m. with the last admission at 5:00 p.m. It is 55 miles from Orlando. Follow I-4 west and take Exit 55. Go south on U.S. Highway 27 for 23 miles, past Eagle Ridge Mall and two traffic lights. Turn left on Mountain Lake Cut Off Road and follow the signs. Small admission fee—Saturday admission is free between 8:00 and 9:00 a.m. Carillon concert daily at 3:00 p.m. No pets, but pet facility available. Great picnicking spots. 115 Tower Boulevard, Lake Wales, Florida 33853-3412
www.boksanctuary.org   **863-676-1408**

Cross Creek

MARJORIE KINNAN RAWLINGS HISTORIC STATE PARK

arjorie Kinnan Rawlings (1896-1953) had tried all kinds of writing—romance novels and gothic stories among other genres—but her editor, Maxwell Perkins, told her it was her letters about her new life near Cross Creek, Florida, that intrigued him the most. Her neighbors didn't know what to make of this New York lady who used good china and silver when

The Marjorie Kinnan Rawlings house, and below, Miss Rawlings in her Cross Creek garden.

serving up meals in her grove house on the edge of the Florida hammock. She spent a lot of time at a typewriter on her screened veranda, writing stories, but they figured it was just her folly. She gained their acceptance and love as she struggled along with them to survive during the leanest years of the Great Depression. In 1938, she published the

Pulitzer Prize-winning novel, *The Yearling*, filled with characters and settings in the Florida scrub. In 1942, she released *Cross Creek*, a nonfiction book about her Florida life.

Eight acres of her property are now a state park. The property includes her grove house, decorated and filled with her things, looking as if she just stepped out and will be back at any minute. Cross Creek is about an hour and fifteen minutes by car from Orlando: a great place to see this "bend in a country road" made famous by a very talented writer.

Between Ocala and Gainesville at 18700 CR-325, Cross Creek, Florida. From Central Florida take the East-West Expressway west to the Florida Turnpike. Take the Turnpike to Exit 309 and merge onto I-75. Take Exit 71 off I-75 and turn right (east) onto Hwy. 326. At U.S. Hwy. 301 turn left (north). (The number changes back and forth between 301 and 441, but just keep going straight.) At C.R. 325 turn left (west) to Cross Creek. Open 9:00 a.m. to 5:00 p.m. every day. Tours available Thursday-Sunday, 10:00 a.m to 4:00 p.m. except August and September. Meet the Friends of the Marjorie Kinnan Rawlings Farm, Inc. at www.afn.org~mkr/index.html. Call **352-466-3672** with questions.

A clouded leopard at the Central Florida Zoo.

THE CENTRAL FLORIDA ZOO

The Central Florida Zoological Park began life as the Sanford Zoo. but it has recently been able to broaden its reach. In 2003, the zoo installed new exhibits for the cougar, the king vulture, and the siamang (that's a kind of ape in the gibbon family, but you knew that, right?). They are hard at work on further expansion in accordance with their master plan, which will turn all 116 acres of the zoo into an even better conservation park than it is now. At the zoo you'll be able to see an alligator and a crocodile up close and learn to tell the difference. There are endangered cats on exhibit, including the cheetah, leopard, and puma, along with more common creatures such as the porcupine and the llama. There are tropical birds to meet, including the hyacinth macaw, the green-winged macaw, and the Panama yellow-crowned amazon. On weekends and holidays you can count on animal demonstrations all over the park that everyone in the family will enjoy.

Open every day 9:00 a.m. to 5:00 p.m., except on Thanksgiving and Christmas Day. Small admission fee. 3755 N.W. Route 17-92, Sanford. Take I-4 to Exit 104. From the west, the exit ramp goes directly onto Route 17-92. Heading east, take the ramp onto Orange, turn left at the traffic signal onto Lake Monroe Road, then right onto Route 17-92. The zoo is less than a mile on the right-hand side of 17-92. Call **407-323-4450** *or log on to: www.centralfloridazoo.org.*

A DAY IN WINTER PARK

Winter Park is one of the prettiest villages in Central Florida, and it remains small enough to enjoy on foot. Visitors from all over the world like to spend at least a day in this little town, founded in the 1880s by New Englanders. The first

thing you will want to do is take the **Winter Park Scenic Boat Tour**, at the foot of Morse Boulevard and Lake Osceola. Then you should hit the museums: the **Cornell Fine Arts Museum**, just steps away on the campus of Rollins College, has one of the largest fine arts collections in the state; the **Albin Polasek Museum** features both the home of and sculpture by the Czech artist; and the **Winter Park Historical Museum** has rotat-

ing exhibits to help acquaint you with the town. Just east of downtown on Aloma Avenue, the **Crealdé School of Art** has exhibits and some terrific student sales. The Park Avenue shops are chic, and Central Park is the place to picnic and relax. On Saturday mornings, the town turns out for the **Winter Park Farmers Market** on New York Avenue. Artsy **Hannibal Square** has an interesting collection of restaurants and shops; and nearby **Winter Park Village** features a 20-screen movie theater and more shops and eateries.

As luck would have it, I've written an entire book about Winter Park—and you'll probably be delighted to learn it is much shorter than this one. **The Absolutely Essential® Guide to Winter Park** can be ordered from any bookstore. Or, send an electronic message to the author at rchaps @msn.com.

Winter Park is adjacent to Orlando. Take I-4 to Exit 87 (Fairbanks Avenue), and travel east on Fairbanks, crossing Route 17-92. At the intersection of Fairbanks and Park Avenue, turn left on Park. You'll find paid, covered parking if you turn right at Park and Lyman Boulevard, or turn left at Park and Morse and you'll find free parking at lots on either side of the street after you cross the railroad tracks.

The Christmas, Florida post office in 1947.

CHRISTMAS, FLORIDA

etween Orlando and Titusville is the little town of Christmas and the nearby park and museum honoring Fort Christmas. The fort and town were named because it was on December 25, 1837, that U.S. soldiers reached the spot and began building the stockade. During the Seminole Wars, the army set up a line of these forts across the middle of the state, a day's march—about 23 miles—apart, as a means of bringing security to the area. Settlements grew around these forts, and when the Seminole Wars ended in the middle of the 19th century, many of these forts evolved into towns.

Christmas, Florida, never got much bigger than that. But its name ensured that its post office would always be a busy place at Christmas time. Just as Loveland, Colorado, set up a remailing program for Valentine's Day, Christmas, Florida, is used to postmarking and remailing thousands of letters each Christmas. The fort has been rebuilt and there is now a small museum.

Christmas, Florida, is east of Orlando on Route 50, about halfway between Orlando and the coast. The park and museum can be found at 1300 Fort Christmas Road. Turn north off the highway at the large Christmas tree (lighted year-round). Fort Christmas Museum is open Tuesday-Saturday, 10:00 a.m. to 5:00 p.m., Sunday, 1:00 p.m. to 5:00 p.m. Closed holidays. **407-568-4149**

Annual festivals:		
Cowboy Reunion	January	Potluck event
Bluegrass Festival	March	Music and crafts
Militia Encampment	March and April	Reenactment at the fort
Old Timers Day	May	Honors seniors
Fort Christmas Homecoming	October	Honors pioneer descendants
Cracker Christmas	December	Craft fair, pioneer life re-enactments, blacksmith, booths and exhibits

Orlando Wetlands Park in Christmas   Tucked away in the countryside surrounding Christmas is the Orlando Wetlands Park, operated by the City of
Orlando. There are 18 miles of trails here for bicycling, walking, bird watching,
jogging, and wildlife photography. The park includes pavilions to provide shade
for picnics as well as benches at various locations along the trails. For cyclists—
especially those with cross-country bikes—it is a nice, easy ride with no hills; but
there isn't much shade along the route either. There are two Seminole "chickees"
(huts) in the park as well.

What in the world is an Orlando Wetlands Park doing out in Christmas? It is a
portion of the Iron Bridge Easterly Wetlands, and it is used by Orlando as a large-
scale man-made wetlands to treat reclaimed water. The wetlands are providing
open space and homes for wildlife, and are being used for water recycling and for
recreation. You can't beat that for a multiuse facility.

*The park is 40 minutes from Orlando. Take Route 50 east to Christmas and at Fort
Christmas Road, turn left (north). Take Fort Christmas Road 2.3 miles to Wheeler
Road and turn right (east). Travel 1.5 miles on Wheeler Road, which is unpaved.
Parking will be on the left. No admission fee. Open from 1/2 hour after sunrise until
1/2 hour before sunset. The park is closed October 1 through January 20. Phone*
407-568-1706 *(ask for Mark Sees) for more information, or log on to*
www.ci.orlando.fl.us *and surf to Orlando Wetlands Park to download a brochure.*

835 A FLORIDA HOME SURROUNDED BY TROPICAL FOLIAGE AND HEDGE OF FLAME VINE

Historic Homes and Museums
THIS OLD HOUSE

Even though Americans didn't start building substantial homes in Florida until the last quarter of the 19th century, very few of these early homes have survived. The Florida climate is pretty rough on houses, and that, combined with the American quest for newness, has created a paucity of living architectural history in Central Florida. Here are a few classics that have been preserved:

The Bradlee-McIntyre House   This home, built in 1884-1885 was originally in Altamonte Springs, and was the winter home of National Bradlee of Boston. Its 13 rooms have been refurnished with period furniture. *Open the second and fourth Sunday of each month, 1:00 p.m. to 4:00 p.m., and the second and fourth Wednesday, 11:00 a.m. to 4:00 p.m., 130 W. Warren Avenue, Longwood. Donations accepted.*   **407-332-0225**

The Casements   This is the former winter home of John D. Rockefeller, whose vacations in Ormond Beach encouraged many of his wealthy friends to follow suit. That, in a roundabout way, led to the first auto race on the beach. The house now includes several museum collections, as well as information about the unusual life of America's original Mr. Moneybags. *Open Monday-Friday, 10:00 a.m. to 2:30 p.m., Saturday, 10:00 a.m. to 11:30 a.m., 25 Riverside Drive, Ormond Beach Donations encouraged.*   **386-676-3216**

DeBary Hall   Built in 1871 by New York wine importer Frederick deBary, this hunting estate is now open for tours.
Thursday-Saturday, 10:00 a.m. to 4:00 p.m, Sunday, noon to 4 p.m.
210 Sunrise Boulevard, DeBary
Donations accepted.   **386-668-3840** *and* **386-736-5953**

Henry A. DeLand House Museum   The home was built on land bought from Henry DeLand by George Hamlin, who developed the Hamlin orange. It was later bought by hat manufacturer John B. Stetson as faculty housing for the school that bears his name. *Open Tuesday-Saturday, noon to 4 p.m., 137 W. Michigan Avenue, DeLand Donations accepted*   **386-740-6813**

Moseley House Museum   Very few of the old structures of Eatonville have survived. The Moseley house is now the second oldest structure in Eatonville, and a tour includes information on the history of this, the first incorporated African American city in the United States. *11 Taylor Avenue, Eatonville*
Open Thursday and Saturday, 11:00 a.m. to 4:00 p.m. Free   **407-622-9382**

Waterhouse Residence   This 1884 residence in Maitland once included a carpentry shop, and now that the home has been restored, includes a museum to its multiple uses. *Open Thursday through Sunday, noon to 4:00 p.m., 820 Lake Lily Drive, Maitland*
$2 per person, $5 per family   **407-644-2451**

THE ENZIAN THEATER

Many of the art house movie theaters across the country are in rehabbed movie palaces in downtown areas. Here is one in perhaps the most charming suburban setting in the country. Located on the grounds of an old estate in Maitland, the Enzian is Central Florida's premier theater dedicated to independent and classic films. No loge seats here: there are tables and chairs and a quick service menu that includes salads, sandwiches, and snacks along with beer and wine,

The theater was founded by Tina Tiedke as a repertory house for classic films. Gradually, it evolved into a theater for first-run independent films—and that has become a cutting-edge business. Now operated by Tina's sister-in-law Sigrid Tiedke, it is a nonprofit business dedicated to film as art. The Enzian is the headquarters of the annual Florida Film Festival and the Brouhaha Film & Video Showcase. It also sponsors free Popcorn Flicks in Winter Park's Central Park on the third Thursday of every month. The showings begin just after dusk, and BYOB—bring your own blanket. Membership in the Enzian allows you to book a table in advance for many of the films, and helps support the programs. Check local listings for what's playing at the Enzian Theater while you're in town. It's bound to be something interesting.

*Take I-4 to Exit 88, Lee Road, and drive east to Route 17-92. Turn left (north) onto 17-92 and drive about a mile. The Enzian will be on your right, surrounded by live oaks. The Enzian is supported in part by the State of Florida, Department of State, Division of Cultural Affairs, the Florida Arts Council, and by United Arts of Central Florida. Call **407-629-1088** for more information on the Enzian. The Movie Line number is **407-629-0054**. Or log on to for www.enzian.org.*

THE MAITLAND ART CENTER

The Maitland Art Center is a combination gallery, museum, and art school. The complex includes 23 separate buildings linked by gardens and courtyards, and features Mayan and Aztec themes in the architecture that give it a very Frank Lloyd Wright-ish look. In fact, it was built in the 1930s by artist Jules André Smith (1880-1959) to house an art colony he founded called the Research Studio. It is now on the National Register of Historic Places, and is considered one of the few surviving examples of "fantasy" architecture in the Southeast. Just coming to see the building is worthwhile. But the center also has a number of significant collections

André Smith 1880-1959

*A painting of a harvest, by André Smith in the collection of the Maitland Art Center.
Photo courtesy of the Maitland Art Center.*

including paintings, etchings, and sculpture by the center's founder, Jules André Smith, as well as from other significant 20th century American print makers and painters. There are workshops, classes, artists-in-residence, and a very nice museum store. Exhibits rotate. The Maitland Art Center also sponsors an annual Children's Art Festival each spring.

The Maitland Art Center with its distinctive look. The "R" over the doorway stands for "Research Studio" the original name of the center. Photos courtesy of the Maitland Art Center.

*Open Monday-Friday 9:00 to 4:30 p.m., Saturday and Sunday noon to 4:30 p.m. Closed holidays. No admission charge, donations requested. 231 West Packwood Avenue, Maitland. Not far from Audubon of Florida's Center for Birds of Prey. Take I-4 to Lee Road (Exit 88), and go east on Lee Road to Route 17-92. Turn left (north) onto 17-92 and drive to Packwood Avenue. Turn left (west) onto Packwood. There is free parking. www.maitartctr.org **407-539-2181***

André Smith in a painting by William Orr, 1962.

IF THE SPIRITS MOVE YOU

Spiritualism—that is, the use of mediums to contact the dead—was a popular trend in the 19th century. In Central Florida there is a historic place founded by spiritualists, just 10 miles north of Sanford. It is called Cassadaga—originally called Camp Cassadaga because the word "camp" was associated with meeting places back then. A fellow named George Colby, from New York, had a spirit medium (that is, a person who talks to you from the world of the dead) and his name was "Seneca." In 1875, it seems "Seneca" guided George Colby to the Central Florida woods and told him it was here that he would set up his spiritualist camp. Colby homesteaded the land, and in 1894, Camp Cassadaga was established by members of the American Spiritualist Association. Cassadaga, which includes 35 acres, was designed to be a resort where spiritualists could gather in the winter and séance together.

The little town hasn't changed much in a hundred years and is now on the National Register of Historic Places. It is still populated by people in the spiritualism business who will be happy to give you a "reading" for a small fee. In the historic houses along the sandy streets, you'll find unusual little book-

A vintage postcard from the days when the city was still called Camp Cassadaga, from the Florida State Archives.

stores full of New Age literature, incense, and crystals. The Cassadaga Hotel is spiritualism central, and when you enter, you'll get the funny feeling you've just walked into a Stephen King novel. Plan to see Cassadaga during at least one of your lifetimes.

To find Cassadaga you could make contact with "Seneca", or you could travel east on I-4 to Exit 114 (S.R. 472). Travel west on S.R. 472 toward Orange City/Deland. Merge right onto C.R. 4101 (Dr. Martin L. King Jr. Drive). Turn right onto Cassadaga Rd (C.R. 4139). Turn right onto Marion Street.

THE WEKIVA RIVER

Wekiwa Springs State Park is set along the Wekiva River: why is that? Wekiwa and wekiva are really the same Indian word spelled two different ways. Both are based on the Creek word for "spring of water"—so Wekiwa Springs is a redundancy, but no one seems to mind. The river begins with a crystal-clear spring in an area that is now part the Orlando suburbs. The spring creates a 16-mile-long river filled with subtropical flora and fauna just 30 minutes north of Orlando's downtown.

Wekiwa Springs State Park The 7,800-acre park has been a popular spot for Floridians to swim and picnic since the 19th century—and Indian mounds show it had a special place in native American history too. At the park, there are canoes to rent, camping, and the best swimming hole in Central Florida. The springs spout 42 million gallons of water daily at 72°F (22.2°C) making them wonderfully refreshing during an Orlando summer day. Canoeing is especially enjoyable because of the wealth of wildlife that surrounds the river: baby alligators sun themselves on logs, turtles, egrets, herons, eagles, owls, deer, and schools of fish will eye you cautiously as you ply your leisurely way down river. Some people report they've seen bears along the river as well. As you paddle, you feel as if you've gone back in time to the Florida of long ago.

Small admission charge, canoe rentals available, pets must be on leash, parking limited to 300 spots. Call **800-326-3521** *to make sure there is room for your vehicle, or to make camping reservations. There are campsites and a few cabins. Also log on to www.reserveamerica.com. Open 365 days of the year. Take I-4 east to Exit 94 and follow the signs to 1800 Wekiwa Circle, Apopka. Directions and map available at www.dep.state.fl.us/parks.*

GONE FISHIN'

T he St. Johns is one of the longest rivers in the United States to flow northward. From its beginnings in Central Florida, it flows about 300 miles north and east to the Atlantic Ocean near Jacksonville. A century ago, steamboats used the river to transport people and goods from Jacksonville to Sanford. Today the St. Johns is a place for fishing and fun.

Hontoon Island State Park A relaxing way to see the St. Johns River is by visiting Hontoon Island State Park. It is just six miles west of DeLand, about an hour or less from Orlando. The only way to the island is by ferry—or by private boat. There is a parking area on the mainland, and the ferry operates from 8:00 a.m. until one hour before sundown. There are campsites and rustic cabins on the island, but I suspect most visitors will just stop in for a day. If you come in the winter months, rent a canoe and paddle around looking for manatees. If you visit in the summer, arrive early in the day before it is too hot, and enjoy watching the wildlife as you cook your breakfast on an open grill. There are ancient Indian mounds to explore, a three-mile self-guided nature trail, and a picnic area with a playground for children. Fishing is not only permitted, it is encouraged: you can catch largemouth bass, bluegills, shellcrackers, and speckled perch. Some people even like to catch catfish. All you need is a fishing license—required for those 16 years of age and older.

BASS FISHING IN FLORIDA

Hontoon Island, 2309 River Ridge Road, DeLand. To find the park take I-4 east from Orlando to Exit 118 (S.R.44). Travel west on S.R. 44 six miles to the Hontoon Island ferry dock. The ferry is free. The island is very near Blue Spring State Park, so it is easy to combine a trip to the spring with a visit to the island. The park is open every day of the year from 8 a.m. until sunset.   **386-736-5309**

STRAWBERRY FESTIVALS FOREVER (AND MORE)

When it's Gladioli Time in Florida.

F lorida is the land of festivals. If something blooms, is harvested, hatches, goes on display, or needs performing, somebody starts a festival honoring it. It may just be because we have such nice weather in Florida. Any excuse for getting together with friends and neighbors is a good one when the sun is shining. These are a sampling of Central Florida's best-known festivals:

Zora Neale Hurston Festival of Arts and Humanities Hurston, the celebrated African American folklorist and writer, is a native of Eatonville, the first incorporated African American city in the nation. Each **January**, the city of Eatonville, just a few miles north of Orlando, celebrates its art and history.   **800-972-3310**

Mount Dora Festival of the Arts This is one of Florida's rare communities that actually have hills! (Perhaps they should have a hill festival?) The art festival, held each year in late **January** and early **February**, attracts hundreds of thousands of people who enjoy walking Mount Dora's quaint streets, full of antique shops and charming eateries.   **352-383-0880**

Florida Strawberry Festival Some of the sweetest strawberries in the nation are too fragile to ship cross-country—but you'll find them at festivals like this one in Plant City, just south of Walt Disney World. Held for 10 days in late **February** and early **March** each year, it is a wonderful community fair.   **813-752-9194**

Winter Park Sidewalk Art Festival Organized beginning in 1960, this three-day festival attracts at least a quarter of a million people each year to pretty Park Avenue and Central Park. One of the premier art festivals in the nation, it is held each year in **March.**   **407-672-6390**

Kissimmee Bluegrass Festival Celebrating traditional American music, from bluegrass and Creole to Texas swing, this three-day **March** event is always a hit— with residents and visitors alike. Held on the grounds of the Silver Spurs Rodeo.
                                                                          813-783-7205

Florida Film Festival The folks at the Enzian Theater in Maitland got this going, and it is now a big event. Usually held in **March** the festival's screenings can be found at theaters all over Orlando. Opening night is almost always at the Enzian, and the awards celebration is often at Universal Studios. Lots of new, independent films, and an excellent cast of stars. The date is subject to change.   **407-629-1088**

Apopka Art and Foliage Festival This Orange County city is known as the "indoor foliage capital of the world," and in 1961, the Apopka Woman's Club began this festival honoring its major industry. Held annually on the fourth weekend in **April** at the Kit Land Nelson Park in Apopka. Call the Apopka Woman's Club for information.
407-884-8911

Orlando's Spring Fiesta in the Park Regional arts and crafts are the focus on the beautiful shores of Orlando's Lake Eola. More than 175 artists take part in this **April** weekend event.   **407-246-2827**

360.   A STRAWBERRY FIELD IN FLORIDA.

Melbourne, Fla.

Melbourne Art Festival Held annually near the end of **April** in this beachside city in Brevard County, this festival salutes both artists and the sea. Only about 40 miles east of Orlando on the Bee Line Expressway.   **321-722-1964**

The Orlando International Fringe Festival An unusual festival for a square town like Orlando, but its "out there" theater, comedy, and performance events are a big hit in downtown Orlando each **May**. Most performances take place at outdoor venues. Lots of nutty fun.   **407-648-0077**

The Zellwood Sweet Corn Festival During World War II, as all of America's industries focused on the war, food shortages required rationing. Farmers in Zellwood, looking for more efficient ways to grow crops, dammed-off areas of Lake Apopka and found the muck that remained was extremely fertile for vegetable crops. Zellwood became known for its wonderful sweet corn. Each **May**, Zellwood's festival honors the "sweetest sweet corn in the nation."
www.zellwoodsweetcornfest.org   **407-886-0014**

Maitland Art Festival Just next door to Winter Park, Maitland is home to the Enzian Theater and the Maitland Art Center. It has two annual art festivals: one in **October** sponsored by the Rotary, and one in **April** sponsored by the Chamber of Commerce. Call the Chamber at **407-644-0741** or the Rotary at **407-263-5218**.

Orlando's Fall Fiesta in the Park This is about four times as big as the Spring Festival in the Park. It begins on the shores of Lake Eola and spreads out onto the streets of downtown Orlando. Held annually in **November**, it is one of the top five outdoor arts and crafts show in Florida.   **407-246-2827**

DeLand Festival of the Arts DeLand is about halfway between Orlando and Daytona Beach, very easy to reach off I-4. It is the home of historic Stetson University—one of the first colleges in the State of Florida. The festival is held each **November** in this historic town.   www.delandfallfestival.com

---

Disney's Festival of the Masters This is worth a mention because it has been going on for 27 years and it is free. (Lots of the festivals are free—but this one's at Disney!) It takes place all around Downtown Disney for three days in **November** and is awash in the usual Disney style.   **407-824-4321**

Bach Festival It began at Winter Park's Rollins College in 1935, and has now expanded beyond its original spring schedule of events. The actual festival continues to be held in **March**, but some of its most beautiful concerts take place in **November** and **December** to mark the Christmas holidays. Internationally known guest stars appear, and Dr. John Sinclair conducts.   **407-646-2182**

Florida's Famous Fountain at Night, Stetson University, Deland, Florida

Be There! Be There! Be There!

NOT A DRAG AT ALL

You've probably heard of Donald G. "Big Daddy" Garlits (b. 1932). If you haven't, now would be a good time to get acquainted with him. He is one of the top American drag racers of all time, so famous that the Smithsonian Museum of American History has his car Swamp Rat XXX on display. Garlits began drag racing in 1950 and won his first major victory in 1955. From that date he just took off, so to speak, and won every award in drag racing. He was the first driver to go 170 mph, then the first to go 180, and so on until, as a grandfather in 2002, he took Swamp Rat XXXIV out of mothballs, souped it up a bit, and drove it to 318.54 mph in 4.76 seconds at the National Hot Rod Association's U.S. Nationals. He was the first to promote women in the sport, and he's been a guest at the White House. He and his wife, Pat, established the International Drag Racing Hall of Fame, with its annual induction ceremony timed to coincide with the Gatornationals in Gainesville. Don Garlits is the Big Daddy of drag racing.

Big Daddy stands in front of the Museum of Drag Racing with the classic Swamp Rat I, which he raced in 1957. Go, Big Daddy!
Photo courtesy of Don Garlits

In 1984, he established the **Don Garlits Museum of Drag Racing** near his home in Ocala, Florida. In 1995, he built a second museum next door to the first called the **Museum of Classic Automobiles**, for his collection of classic cars. It is all a not-for-profit operation because that is the kind of guy Don Garlits is.

Garlits advertises this attraction as "just one hour north of Orlando." Considering his history, you might want to plan on giving yourself a little more time to get there: the distance between Orlando and the Museum of Drag Racing is 74 miles.

The Don Garlits Museum of Drag Racing,13700 S.W. 16th Avenue, Ocala. Take I-75 to Exit 67, and exit onto S.R.484. At the intersection of S.R.484 and 475A (S.W. 16th Avenue), turn left and you'll be at the museum. Entrance fees are small. Both museums open every day of the year except Christmas, from 9:00 a.m. to 5:00 p.m. More information at www.garlits.com. **877-271-3278**

Leu Gim Gong and his rooster "March."
Courtesy of the West Volusia Historical Society.

LUE GIM GONG
THE CITRUS WIZARD

Lue Gim Gong had a nursery in DeLand, Florida that was the envy of his neighbors. In 1911, he received the Silver Wilder Medal from the U.S. Department of Agriculture for an orange variety he hybridized—called the "Lue Gim Gong"—that ripened in the early fall and was resistant to cold. He also created a light pink raspberry, and a juiceless aromatic grapefruit. His neighbors called him the "Citrus Wizard."

How did a man born in Canton, China, end up owning a nursery in Central Florida at the turn of the 20th century? Lue moved with an uncle to San Francisco

Leu Gim Gong with the Dumvilles in DeLand, about 1886.
Courtesy of the West Volusia Historical Society.

in 1872, when the railroads were hiring Chinese laborers. We don't know why, but Leu didn't stay in the West, and somehow worked his way east, where the teenager took a job at a shoe factory in North Adams, Massachusetts. There he became ill, and was taken in by Fannie Burlingame, a well-off maiden lady who had seen Lue at her church. With her help, Lue regained his health, became an American citizen, and was baptized a Christian.

"Mother Fannie," as Leu called his benefactress, moved to DeLand, Florida in 1886, to be near her sister Cynthia and Cynthia's husband William Dumville, who operated a citrus grove. Leu moved to DeLand too, and worked with Mr. Dumville in his grove. The young Cantonese was the son of Chinese farmers and it turned out he had a knack for growing things.

This is the medal from the U.S. Department of Agriculture won by Leu Gim Gong.
Courtesy of the West Volusia Historical Society.

"Mother Fannie" returned regularly to her home in the North but Leu remained in DeLand, growing and hybridizing.

During the big freeze of 1894-1895 he lost all of his trees, but when the weather warmed Leu replanted the groves. William Dumville died in 1895, and then Fannie Burlingame died in 1903. The family left Leu the property in DeLand and $10,000. For the rest of his life, he lived alone on the property with his two horses "Baby" and "Fannie" and his rooster "March" and continued his work. Every Sunday, he held prayer services in a gazebo behind his house, and many of his neighbors grew to know him through his Sunday meetings. He died in 1925 and was buried in DeLand's Oakdale cemetery.

For five years, his grave had no marker. Then, in 1930, a member of the New York Historical Society collected the money to have one made. In 1999, Mrs. Hawtense Conrad donated the money for a new marker that incorporated the original 1930 headstone. DeLand has now dedicated a Leu Gim Gong Memorial, which incorporates a bust of Lue and a small gazebo to honor the man who lived such a solitary life in a strange land, and had such talent in the garden.

The "Citrus Wizard" with his benefactress Fannie Burlingame, and her sister Cynthia Dumville. Courtesy of the West Volusia Historical Society.

For more information on the Lue Gim Gong Memorial, contact the West Volusia Historical Society, Inc. 137 West Michigan Avenue, DeLand, Florida.
386-740-6813

BEAUTIES ON THE BEACH IN FLORIDA

F43

Cocoa, Fla. Ole

BEACHED

SOUTH FROM OCEAN PIER,

nt and Indian River.

SHOWING WIDTH OF MOST WONDERFUL BEACH IN THE WORLD. DAYTONA BEACH. FLA.

222

ʙᴇᴀᴄʜᴇᴅ

820   SURF-BATHING IN FLORIDA

"THE FUN COAST" AND "THE SPACE COAST"

Central Florida's Atlantic coast beaches are in two counties: Volusia County, known as "The Fun Coast," and Brevard County known as "The Space Coast." Brevard County is south of Volusia, and from the southern tip of Brevard to the northern tip of Volusia, there are more than a hundred miles of some of the broadest and most beautiful beaches in the world. The region includes Daytona Beach, where racing began a century ago, right on the beach; the Kennedy Space Center, home of the space shuttle and all the moon launches; and Port Canaveral, now the busiest cruise port in this hemisphere. All of these are within an hour to an hour and a half of Orlando.

Daytona Beach and the other Volusia County attractions are reached via I-4 East. The Brevard County attractions are at the eastern end of the Bee Line Expressway.

When you visit Central Florida's beaches, you are closer to the equator than in most of the rest of the United States. This means the angle of the sunlight is more direct and your skin will sunburn more quickly. So, slather on the sunscreen with the high SPF, and limit the time you spend sun bathing until you see how well you fare.

The natural beauty of Florida's beaches has been well preserved. Make sure you join in the effort and leave nothing behind but your footprints. In the interest of the local economy, the only other thing you are encouraged to leave behind is a little of your money.

The Fun Coast

"THE WORLD'S MOST FAMOUS BEACH"

D aytona Beach is named after Mathias Day, who bought more than 2,000 acres of land along the Halifax River in 1871. A year later, he found he couldn't keep up his payments and lost the property. Still in 1876, when the city incorporated, it called itself "Day-tona" in honor of one of its earliest pioneers.

Mathias Day notwithstanding, Daytona Beach will forever be associated with the automobile. Why? Daytona Beach is one of the rare beaches in the United States that are 500 feet wide at low tide and have sand that is smooth and hard-packed. Innovators like Henry Ford figured out how to produce automobiles much more quickly than cities and counties figured out how to afford to build good roads. So, in the early part of the 20th century, when cars were getting better but roads were not, drivers on vacation began to discover Daytona Beach. The beach turned out to be the best "road" they'd ever driven on, and Daytona's tradition of allowing cars on the beach began.

Once you put cars together with a wide, safe roadway—even one made out of sand—you can count on the fact that there will soon be a race. And that's just what happened in 1902, when Ransom Olds (1864-1950)—the builder of the

The World Famous Daytona Beach, Florida

K5999

The Line up DAYTONA BEACH, Fla.   3196.

Amateurs lead the way initially on the beach, but as the speeds got higher, car owners hired professional racers to drive their vehicles. Postcard courtesy of the Florida State Archives.

Oldsmobile—and Alexander Winton (1860-1932)—who called his car "The Bullet"—raced their automobiles down the sands of Ormond Beach, just north of Daytona. According to legend, the cars reached the amazing speed of 57 mph that day, and the gentlemen's race ended in a tie. It was the beginning of racing on the sands of Ormond Beach and Daytona Beach that would continue for another half a century.

William H.G. France entered the sport in the 1930s. He bought a service station near the beach, and it turned out to be a place where drivers liked to hang out. When the races needed a promoter, he stepped in and turned out to be great at promoting the sport he loved. After World War II, he could see that the expanding business of racing needed something better than a beach to race on, and he built the Daytona International Speedway, which opened with the first Daytona 500 on February 22, 1959. Bill France died in 1992, and now, two more generations of the France family of Daytona Beach are running the business.

Daytona Beach is probably the glitziest of Central Florida's beach towns. It hosts lots of parties, and when you see it, you'll recognize it as a party town. Visiting Daytona Beach today means taking in a race or a tour at the Speedway; cruising through town on your Harley for Bike Week: and, incidentally, enjoying the sun and the surf at the famous beach. Daytona Beach hosts Speedweeks

Daytona Beach Area Convention and Visitors Bureau
The CVB has a wonderful Web site with everything from the daily temperature and tide tables to the latest events all over the "Fun Coast."
www.daytonabeach.com   **800-854-1234**

Daytona Beach Boardwalk and Main Street Pier
Beach-y arcades, souvenir stands, and observation tower.
100 Main Street   **386-238-1212**

Museum of Arts and Sciences
1040 Museum Boulevard
www.Moas.org   **386-255-0285**

Seaside Music Theater
176 North Beach Street and 1200 West International Speedway Boulevard
www.seasidemusictheater.org   **800-854-5592**

(January/February), Bike Week (February/March), Spring Break (March), the Pepsi 400 (July), and Biketoberfest (October), and that's not even a complete list of the events. In the 21st Century, there are still places you can drive on the World's Most Famous Beach, with one proviso: keep your top speed under 10 mph.

It wasn't long before cars began to be designed just for racing.
Postcard courtesy of the Florida State Archives.

The Fun Coast
DAYTONA INTERNATIONAL SPEEDWAY

W illiam H.G. France (1909-1992) is one of the legends of auto racing, and without him Daytona Beach would likely have remained a quiet little beach town. It was in Daytona Beach in 1948 that France and some friends founded the National Association of Stock Car Auto Racing—NASCAR. In 1959, France built the Daytona International Speedway, which opened the throttle on stock car racing, made millionaires of practically everyone associated with the sport, and turned Daytona Beach into a motor sports mecca.

The 480-acre Daytona International Speedway now hosts race events under the aegis of NASCAR, the American Motorcycling Association, and the World Karting Association, which take place year-round. When there is a break in the schedule, concerts and other arena events fill the seats. Even if there is not a race going on during your visit, a trip to the Speedway is a required pilgrimage for anyone who loves racing.

Photo courtesy of ISC.

Now, the speedway offers a permanent attraction called **Daytona USA**, a sort of indoor theme park for race fans. It opened July 5, 1996, and has all kinds of treats on hand. One is Sir Malcolm Campbell's expertly restored "Bluebird V," the 12,000-pound race car with the V-12 Rolls Royce engine that went 276.82 mph on the sands of Daytona Beach in 1935, to set the world speed record. There are interactive exhibits and much more, and if the weather permits, there are also tours of the track.

Daytona USA. Photo courtesy of ISC.

*The Daytona International Speedway is 52 miles from Orlando. Take I-4 East, and when you reach the outskirts of Daytona Beach go straight onto S.R.400 E, turn left onto Beville Road, and take the on ramp to I-95 North. Merge onto I-95 and take Exit 261 (U.S.92) toward DeLand/Daytona Beach. Keep right at the fork. Merge onto U.S.92 E and look for the entrance at 1801 West International Speedway Boulevard. Daytona USA is located at the Speedway and is open 9:00 a.m. to 7:00 p.m. every day except Christmas Day, extended hours during racing events. For speedway tickets call **386-253-7223**. General information can be found at **386-254-2700**.*

Automobile Races.   Ormond, Fla.

THE BIRTHPLACE OF SPEED

D aytona Beach gets all the attention, but the first beach race—actually the first few years of beach racing—took place in adjacent Ormond Beach. The reason the races began at all is that Ormond Beach was a fancy resort town in the late 19th and early 20th centuries, and it attracted wealthy men like Ransom Olds and Alex Winton to the Hotel Ormond in the winter. Once there, the fancy gents had time on their hands, a nice stretch of beach out the window, and their newfangled cars in the parking lot. It was inevitable that they could resist everything but the temptation to take those babies out for a spin to see how fast they'd go.

Ormond Beach is now a community of 35,000 people, with beaches just as wide as Daytona's. The sands tend to be a little less crowded and the native style a little more reserved. Ormond Beach continues to have historic racing sites for buffs to visit, as well as a lot of good restaurants and resorts. Each Thanksgiving, it holds a celebration honoring its role as the "Birthplace of Speed."

For more information on things to see and do in Ormond Beach, contact the Ormond Beach Chamber of Commerce at www.ormondchamber.com, or contact the Daytona Beach Area Convention and Visitors Bureau, at 126 East Orange Avenue, Daytona Beach, Florida. **800-854-1234**

LIGHTING THE WAY

Just 10 miles south of Daytona Beach is one of just a few remaining 19th century lighthouses to have all its original buildings intact—the Ponce de Leon Inlet Lighthouse, built in the 1880s. The Spanish were the first to explore this part of the Florida coast, but they found the inlet treacherous, and the climate inauspicious. They called the place *los Mosquitos* for unfortunately obvious reasons and left it pretty much alone. The first lighthouse built on the spot, in 1835, never became operational and fell into the sea in 1836 after it was hit by a hurricane and attacked by the Seminole Indians. Seminole leader Coacoochee, reportedly wore one of the lighthouse reflectors as a headdress at the battle of Dunlawton. Under the circumstances, it seemed wise to abandon the lighthouse idea for a while.

Mosquito Inlet Light House on the Halifax River, near Daytona Beach, Florida.

In 1883, a project to build a new lighthouse began, and on November 1, 1887 the kerosene lamp at the Mosquito Inlet Lighthouse was lighted for the first time. In 1927, the name of Mosquito Inlet was changed to Ponce de Leon Inlet, and the lighthouse received the more charming name too. By 1970, lighthouses had grown passé, and the Coast Guard abandoned the old station. Two years later, some thoughtful locals formed the Ponce de Leon Inlet Lighthouse Preservation Association and began to restore and manage this historic treasure. The lighthouse, once called "the most beautiful and best proportioned tower in the district," is now on the National Register of Historic Places.

The Ponce de Leon Inlet Lighthouse is open every day of the year except Christmas. From Memorial Day through Labor Day, 10:00 a.m. to 9:00 p.m. In the fall and winter, closing is at 5:00 p.m. 4931 South Peninsula Drive, Ponce Inlet. The three keepers' buildings have been turned into museums. Small admission charge.
www.ponceinlet.org   **386-761-1821**

Smyrna Yacht Club, New Smyrna Beach

New Smyrna Beach The Timucuan Indians left a great deal of evidence of their lives at the Florida Coast. Near New Smyrna Beach, they shelled and ate so many oysters at their camps that the shells created a mound of 33,000 cubic yards, covering 2 acres and rising 50 feet in the air. The Spanish built a mission here in the early 16th century, but hostile natives, and hostile mosquitos, caused them to abandon it. In 1769, Scotsman Andrew Turnbull recruited Greek and Italian citizens to help him homestead his 101,000-acre land grant. Perhaps because of the Mediterranean origin of the settlers, the settlement was called New Smyrna, after the Greek locale. It fell victim to the same hazards that had preyed on the Spanish. In the late 19th century, when the railroad arrived, settlement began again, and by 1903, the city of New Smyrna Beach was incorporated. Visitors today can enjoy 13 miles of beaches with a definite family-friendly orientation. Nearby, there are the ruins of the area's first sugar mill, off Route 44 and Old Mission Road. The big Indian shell mound, called Turtle Mound, is located 9 miles south of town within the Canaveral National Seashore. The Eldora State House is also in the park. It is the restored home of a once prosperous coastal community.

New Smyrna Beach is north of Cape Canaveral, south of Daytona Beach. Exit 249A off I-95. Contact the Canaveral National Seashore at **386-428-3384**. *New Smyrna Beach Visitors' Bureau, 2242 State Road 44, New Smyrna Beach, Florida.*
www.volusia.com   **800-541-9621**

Canaveral National Seashore Canaveral National Seashore is a federal park that extends 24 miles along the Florida coast, south of New Smyrna Beach. It includes 58,000 acres that stretch from southern Volusia County to northern Brevard. More than 1,000 species of plants and 310 species of birds are found within its borders. The land was originally set aside for NASA when the Kennedy Space Center was built, but not all of it was needed and this section became a national park. The beaches are beautiful and undeveloped and tend to be less packed with crowds than those to both the north and south of the park in commercial areas. Off the beach, there are nature trails, Indian mounds, visiting manatees, campsites, horseback trails, pontoon boat cruises, and interpretative walks. You'll want to bring your own picnic, as there are no restaurants within the park. There are no RV hook-ups either and camping is fairly primitive. During shuttle launches, parts of the park may be closed for security reasons.

Just FYI: for a while, there were some determined naturists hanging out, so to speak, at Playalinda Beach within the park. They were frequently given "citations" (where did they put them, I wonder?) by red-faced park rangers, and have apparently been discouraged, but you never know. Depending upon your point of view (in this case, literally) this may either attract our repel you. Which reminds me of the story my grandmother used to tell about the man who streaked nude at the senior citizens' home. "What was that?" asked one grandmother. "I don't know," said her friend. "But whatever it was, it needed ironing."

South on A1A, 9 miles from New Smyrna Beach. Or, north from Titusville, I-95 to SR-406 (Exit 80), SR-406 east to SR-402 east to park entrance. Open 6:00 a.m. to 6:00 p.m, November-March; 6:00 a.m. to 8:00 p.m., April-October. Lifeguards Memorial Day-Labor Day. Visitors Center, closed Christmas Day only.

The Space Coast
REACHING FOR THE STARS

D rive east from Orlando toward Cape Canaveral and the Kennedy Space Center, and certain images will come to mind: President John F. Kennedy's speech setting the goal of reaching the moon "before this decade is out"; the Mercury astronauts with *The Right Stuff*; Neil Armstrong's "one small step"; Apollo 13's safe return; the tragedies of *Challenger* and *Columbia*; NASA engineers with their crew cuts and short-sleeved shirts. Florida's Kennedy Space Center at Cape Canaveral has seen good days and bad in the 40 years that Americans have reached for the stars. On all days, it is a landmark to the dreams we dream.

Brevard County is proud to call itself the Space Coast. NASA employs 1,800 people at the Kennedy Space Center, and 12,000 more people work there as contractors. The ongoing series of launches from the Cape since the 1950s have transformed the world we live in: satellite phones and satellite television; live hurricane tracking from earth orbit; global positioning devices in Army tanks and civilian SUVs—none of this would have been possible without the space program. There are lots of things to see and do along the Space Coast. One of the best is to salute the area itself and its important place in the history of exploration.

From Wally Schirra's "man in a can" Mercury 8 capsule, to the reusable space shuttle Endeavour (launching 6/21/93), America's history in space is irrevocably linked to Florida's Brevard County. Photos courtesy of NASA.

"WE ARE GO..."

Launch Viewing If the weather is clear, you can see almost all of the Kennedy Space Center launches from Orlando. Just check up on the launch schedule, find a comfortable place in the Orlando area in which to stand or sit looking directly east, and once the rocket or shuttle clears the tree line, you'll get a good view of the vehicle headed toward "the universe and beyond." Night launches—especially night launches of the shuttle—are especially dramatic, and impossible to miss if you are out-of-doors.

Still, the viewing is better the closer you get to the Cape. The best viewing sites in Brevard County are: the shores of the Indian River in downtown Titusville; the Cocoa Beach Pier; or any of the beaches along the coast south of Port Canaveral. There is really just one good route from Orlando to Brevard County, and that is the Bee Line Expressway. Traffic can be especially heavy on the Bee Line and on all the roads surrounding the viewing areas during space shuttle launches, so plan accordingly. After the loss of the space shuttle *Columbia*, the shuttle schedule was put on hold. When the schedule resumes, you can expect especially large crowds for the first few years—for both liftoffs and landings. In the meantime, there is a full schedule of unmanned rockets blasting off from the Cape—some with NASA payloads, some with commercial payloads, and others with super-secret Department of Defense payloads. Every launch is a spectacular sight.

The shuttle returns to flight with the launch of Discovery from pad 39-B at KSC on September 29, 1988. Photo courtesy of NASA.

A full launch schedule is available at www.space-coast.com. Or call NASA at **321-867-4636**, or **800-KSC-INFO (800-572-4636)** for a recording of planned launches. Remember: even after the shuttle schedule has resumed, shuttle launches are frequently delayed at the last minute, so don't be disappointed if a liftoff you would like to see has to be rescheduled.

Returning safely home. The space shuttle Atlantis touches down on Runway 15 at the KSC for the conclusion of STS-86, October 6, 1997.

Kennedy Space Center Visitor Complex   If you have seen the Smithsonian Air and Space Museum—the most popular museum in Washington, DC—this is right up there with it in terms of high quality exhibits about the triumphant U.S. space program. It has the Smithsonian beat on one important count—the KSC Visitor Complex has the space shuttle launch pad sitting right next door. From the complex you can catch a bus tour of the restricted areas, or take a special tour of the old Mercury, Gemini, and Apollo launch pads. There are three IMAX® films showing, and enough space hardware to engross any fan of space flight for hours on end. There are three restaurants at the complex too. The astronaut memorial has become a touching place to honor all the astronauts lost during the program—most recently the members of the crew of the space shuttle *Columbia*.

The U.S. Astronaut Hall of Fame   This was set up by the Mercury Seven Foundation—an organization founded by the original seven Mercury astronauts to encourage scientific achievement and scholarships. In 2002, the Hall of Fame was bought by the Kennedy Space Center Visitor Complex, and both are now operated by the same company. It is not far from the KSC Visitor Complex, and many tickets now include a tour of both facilities.

The KSC Visitor Complex is open 9:00 a.m. to 5:30 p.m. every day except Christmas Day. There are some restrictions on launch days. From Orlando, take S.R. 528 (the Bee Line Expressway) east. At S.R. 407, head toward the KSC and Titusville; S.R. 407 dead-ends at S.R. 405. Follow the signs for the KSC, and travel 9 miles on S.R. 405. The Kennedy Space Center Visitor Complex will be on your right. **321-449-4444.** *Launch information at* **800-KSC-INFO (800-572-4636)**. *Tickets available at the Complex, or log on to www.kennedyspacecenter.com.*

CRUISIN'

P ort Canaveral began by serving cargo ships in 1955, and is now the busiest cruise port in the Western Hemisphere with service—at last count—from at least nine cruise lines. The Disney Cruise Line has service from Port Canaveral on its two ships, the Disney *Magic* and the Disney *Wonder*, and has vacation packages that include days at its theme parks, bus service to Port Canaveral, and a cruise on one of the Disney ships.

If you would like to plan a cruise out of Port Canaveral, the best thing to do is contact a travel agent who specializes in sea vacations. If you are Internet savvy, you can do a lot of your research on line. The cruise ships that call Port Canaveral home offer a range of experiences, from overnight trips, to weekends in the Caribbean, to much longer vacations at sea. When and if you make reservations, remember that June 1 to November 30 is the season for hurricanes in the Atlantic, and cruises have been known to face cancellation or adjustments in their itineraries based on these forces of nature. If you've read Sebastian Junger's *The Perfect Storm* (or seen the movie), you'll agree that such modifications are preferable to the potential alternatives.

The port is just 45 miles east of Orlando International Airport, an easy ride on S.R. 528, the Bee Line Expressway. If cruising is not your thing, or if, like Samuel Johnson (1709-1784), you believe: "Being in a ship is being in a jail, with the chance of being drowned ... " consider the fun of just watching the ships come and go. Get yourself a good pair of field glasses, head for the port, find a good vantage point, and enjoy observing the voluntarily incarcerated.

> *For information call* **888-PortCan** **(888-767-8226)**, *or log on to:* www.portcanaveral.org.

PASSENGER CAPACITY 780   P. & O. TURBINE PASSENGER STEAMSHIP "FLORIDA"   387 FEET LONG
SPEED 19 KNOTS PER HOUR   56 FEET WIDE

I DREAM OF COCOA

n 1948, the federal government sent specialists to Brevard County to reopen the Banana River Naval Air Station—renamed Patrick Air Force Base—and to begin setting up the Joint Long Range Proving Ground at Cape Canaveral— later renamed the John F. Kennedy Space Center. Since then, Cocoa Beach and the surrounding towns have grown and prospered. The **Cocoa Beach Pier** is home to four restaurants and, locals say, the best launch viewing in the area. **Olde Cocoa Village** is the restored downtown of Cocoa, with cobbled streets, antique shops, and Porcher House, a historic grove house that is open for tours. The **Brevard Museum of Science and Natural History**, in Cocoa, has native American exhibits, and provides walking tours of Cocoa Village. The nearby City of Melbourne features both the new **Brevard Zoo** and the **Brevard Museum of Art and Science**. The Montreal Expos hold spring training in March at **Space Coast Stadium**, and locals and visitors alike enjoy events at the **Maxwell King Center for the Performing Arts**.

The King Center for the Performing Arts features shows on stage and monthly art exhibits in the Harris Corporation Art Gallery. Each season brings top artists to the stage. For information on performances, call **321-242-2219**, *or log on to* www.kingcenter.com. *For membership information call* **321-634-3781**.

On the shores of the Indian River.
Postcard courtesy of the Florida State Archives.

This vintage postcard looks like a painting by Georges Seurat. No?
Courtesy of the Florida State Archives.

Along the Space Coast
BEAUTIFUL BEACHES

group called the Clean Beaches Council releases its list of the most pristine beaches in the United States each year, and of the 90 beaches so honored in recent years, half are in Florida. That makes Florida the No. 1 beautiful beach state in the nation. In Central Florida, the beaches that received the highest ratings are all in Brevard County, along Florida's Space Coast. They are:

Cape Canaveral Cherie Down Park, Indialantic Boardwalk Beach, Cocoa Beach Alan Shepard Park, Melbourne Beach Ocean Park, and Melbourne Beach Spessard Holland Park.

These beaches topped the list for cleanliness, safety, and environmental preservation. People from other parts of the United States and from other countries—where some beaches are private, and may require a "membership" or a "beach tag"—might be interested to know that all the beaches mentioned above are public, free, and kept beautiful by local governments and by the citizens who use them. They give the rest of Florida's coast—and the rest of the world—a real standard to shoot for.

Endangered and Threatened
SEA TURTLES

I t isn't just humans who flock to the Florida seaside in convention-sized groups. Each summer, Florida beaches host the largest gathering of nesting sea turtles in the United States. These turtles live in the sea and swim to the surface to breathe oxygen. Each year, from April to September, the females come ashore to lay their eggs on the beaches where they were born. Since some of these reptiles weigh as much as 700 pounds, spotting one as it lumbers along is definitely a memorable experience.

All six species of sea turtles that make their homes in the coastal waters of the United States are protected under the 1973 Endangered Species Act. These are the green turtle, hawksbill turtle, Kemp's ridley, leatherback, loggerhead and Olive ridley turtles. Ninety percent of the nesting of all these seagoing creatures takes place on the east coast of Florida.

Florida's Space Coast is also home to the first sea turtle refuge in the United States, the Archie Carr National Wildlife Refuge established by Congress in 1989. Stretching from Melbourne Beach 20 miles south to Wabasso Beach, this refuge is closely monitored to protect the sea turtle nests from damage by both human poachers and animal predators. Still, these big turtles produce such tiny hatchlings that biologists esti-

Sea turtle photos by Jim Angy

mate only one in a thousand survives to reach maturity.

Driving automobiles and all-terrain vehicles (ATVs) on the beach can destroy sea turtle nests. Lights on beachside homes and businesses confuse both the nesting turtles and their hatchlings and keep them from returning safely to the sea. Yet, people living on the coast need lights at night for safety. Many Florida beaches have traditionally been open to vehicles, and businesses fear the economic impact of closing them. Balancing the needs of conservation with the needs of the growing Florida population will be an important challenge in the years ahead.

Hatchlings are so much smaller than adult sea turtles that only about one in a thousand survive.

During the nesting season people who live along the Central Florida coast are asked to extinguish external lighting that is visible from the beach. Beaches that usually allow driving, restrict it during the nesting season. Be aware that if restrictions are

This is a scene you don't see anymore. All six species of sea turtles are protected by federal law. Postcard courtesy of the Florida State Archives.

in place, there are very good reasons for them. If you find the regulations bother-some, why not try to learn more about the turtles and their habitat before you make up your mind? It isn't every day that you'll be able to see a reptile the size of a small Volkswagen move slowly into view, looking for a place to nest. Not unless you are lucky enough to make your home along the Florida coast.

There are a couple of dozen organizations with permits to conduct public sea tur-tle walks during nesting season, and since most of the nesting takes place at night most of the tours are at night too. The Florida Fish and Wildlife Conservation Commission monitors the walks and has a list of them on its Web site at www.flori-daconservation.org/psm/turtles/education. Look for the turtle walk map. The Sea Turtle Preservation Society is another excellent resource. You can reach the STPS at **321-676-1701** *and at www.seaturtlespacecoast.org. Finally try www.cccturtle.org. It is a really dandy Web site produced by the Caribbean Conservation Corporation and has lots of helpful information about sea turtles.*

A terrific CD-Rom "flip book" about sea turtles is available, produced by Florida conservationists Marge Bell, Jim Angy, and Matt MacQueen. My thanks to them for their assistance in my research and for the loan of the photographs that appear here. To learn about their "flip book," log on to www.stillnature.com.

Headin' home. A female sea turtle has made her nest and as the tracks show, she's headed back to the sea.

Disney's Vero Beach Resort
QUIET TIME

ea turtle walks are among the featured activities at one of the prettiest resorts on Central Florida's East Coast. It is Disney's Vero Beach Resort, located south of the Space Coast, just 10 miles north of the town of Vero Beach, with its face to the sea and its back surrounded by Indian River orange groves. When Disney bought the land in the 1990s, it was reportedly the largest remaining stretch of Florida beachfront property still in private hands.

It is what Disney calls a Vacation Club Resort, the Disney version of a time-share resort. But you don't have to join the Vacation Club to visit. There are 112 rooms in the main building, and 60 villas. The large villas facing the ocean are stand-alone

structures that are larger than most homes. Each villa has multiple bedrooms and baths downstairs and an upstairs that is a spacious all-in-one family room and kitchen.

This is a very un-Disney-like place. Yes, there is a nine hole golf course, a croquet lawn, a pool with a slide, two restau-rants, a bar facing the sea, and tennis and basketball courts. But everything is very low key. The resort is isolated from busy roadways, crowds, and glitz. In the evenings, Cast Members tell stories about Florida's Treasure Coast by a beachside campfire. In sea turtle nesting season, there are guided nature walks. The noisiest thing you'll hear at Disney's Vero Beach Resort is the sound of poolside laughter, and in the distance, the quiet murmur of the sea.

Disney's Vero Beach Resort, 9250 Island Grove Terrace, Vero Beach, Florida 32963. From Central Florida, take The Bee Line Expressway (S.R. 528) east to I-95. Follow I-95 South, to Exit 156 (S.R. 512 East). Turn left (east) on S.R. 512 and drive 6.5 miles to U.S. 1. Turn right (south) on U.S. 1 and drive to S.R. 510. Turn left (east) on 510 to A1A. At A1A turn right (south). The resort is immediately on the left. Directions from all over Florida at http://dvc.disney.go.com. *Reservations at* **407-939-7775**.

Orlando Fla, Nov. 20. 1924.
Friend John,
This is the land of
Sunshine and flowers,
I am having a
great time, hope you
are all well, this
leaves Me in good
health, weather is
fine, about 75. this
afternoon,
a Friend,
M. Slater,
Orlando
Fla,

E. C. KROPP CO.— MILWAUKEE

NOV 20
9 PM
1924
ORLANDO
FLA.

Mr John Lyttle
Stoneboro,
Pa,
R.F.D.# 1,.

Gre

Dr. Phillips is the Largest Individual Grower of Oranges, Grapefruit and Tangerines in the World

DR. PHILLIPS' PACKING HOUSE at

The Kind We Raise in Our State

ODDS AND ENDS

878   ALL DRESSED UP TO MEET YOU IN FLORIDA

ODDS AND ENDS

CHRISTMAS IN ORLANDO

P eople who've had enough white (or rainy) Christmases to last a lifetime often spend the holiday in Orlando, where they enjoy having a sunny Christmas instead. The theme parks salute the holiday spirit too: you'll find the **Macy's Holiday Parade** at Universal Orlando; **Wholiday Whobilation™ of Grinchmas™** at Universal Islands of Adventure; the **Norman Rockwell Holiday Showcase** at SeaWorld; the **Osborne Family Spectacle of Lights** at Disney MGM Studios (on hiatus 2003); **Mickey's Very Merry Christmas Party** at Disney's Magic Kingdom; and **Holidays Around the World** at Epcot. Leu Gardens in Orlando holds an annual **Holiday Pops Concert** (www.leugardens.org or **407-246-2620**); International Drive decks its halls with the **I-Drive Fantasy of Lights Celebration**; and Kissimmee provides 20 tons of snow, carriage rides, carolers, and fireworks at its **Kissimmee**

Christmas, Florida preparing for its annual Christmas onslaught of mail, 1947. Photo courtesy of the Florida State Archives.

Holiday Extravaganza (**800-333-5477** or www.floridakiss.com). Winter Park has its annual tree lighting ceremony just after Thanksgiving, in Winter Park's Central Park. The town of Christmas, Florida, holds its Christmas Festival the first weekend in December, an event that includes a holiday crafts fair and tours of Fort Christmas. While you're there, you can drop your Christmas cards in the mailbox and have yourself a merry little Christmas postmark. (Call **407-568-4149** for more information.)

GONE FISHIN' (PART TWO)
OR
HOW TO GET A FISHING LICENSE IN FLORIDA

etting a fishing license is not a difficult thing to do in Florida. However, the laws governing a fishing license are quite complex indeed. There are separate licenses for freshwater fishing and saltwater fishing. There are resident and non-resident licenses. There are different rules for people who are under 16, over 65, members of the armed services, and Georgia residents

---

You can read the details by logging on to:
http://floridafisheries.com

You can acquire a Florida fishing license by telephone, though there is a small surcharge for doing so. With a major credit card in hand call:
888-486-8356 or 888-347-4356.

You can buy an instant fishing license at:
www.eAngler.com

The most economical place to buy a fishing license is at any Florida county tax collector's office. If you don't know where to find one, you can buy a fishing license at many sporting goods stores where fishing equipment is sold. All the money generated by the fishing license fees goes to the Florida Fish and Wildlife Conservation Commission to provide for sustained use of Florida's fish and wildlife.

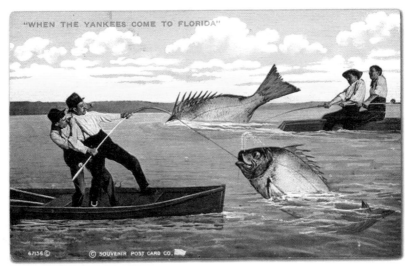
"WHEN THE YANKEES COME TO FLORIDA"

THE FLORIDA ARCHIVIST

D r. Dorothy Dodd (1902-1994) was the State of Florida's first archivist and it is thanks to her diligent and joyous work that the state's library has the wonderful collection it does. She was appointed to her post in 1941, and served as state librarian from 1952 to 1965. With no budget to speak of she acquired and catalogued 15,000 items for the Florida Collection of the state library. Everything

from territorial records to old tax rolls, to negatives from a Tallahassee photographer's attic, were gathered up by Dr. Dodd as the treasures of history she knew they were.

In 1986, when she was 84 years old, Dr. Dodd was inducted into the Florida Women's Hall of Fame. The State Library of Florida now houses its Florida Collection in the Dorothy Dodd Room at the state library in Tallahassee.

Florida State Archivist Dorothy Dodd (at right) getting help from a student. They aren't doing their laundry: they are ironing archival papers! 1953 photo courtesy of the Florida State Archives.

All her life, she took photographs throughout Florida of things in nature she found of interest: a baby gator crossing a highway, pelicans on the wing, wildflowers she found on her hikes that are now very rare, and much more. Because she left this collection of 644 slides to the state archives, I've been able to make use of some of those photos in this book. You'll probably feel as if you got to know Dr. Dodd, just a bit, by the pictures she took; but I, for one, am sorry I didn't get the chance to meet her. She died at the age of 92 in 1994.

A wild violet (left) and a zephyr lily, Florida wildflowers photographed by Dorothy Dodd.

Notice how the clouds avoid blocking the sunlight over Florida?
Isn't that nice? Photo courtesy of NASA.

SAYING GOODBYE

I hope you've learned quite a lot about Orlando and Central Florida in this book. You now know that the Orlando area is home to the space shuttle fleet and to the only launch pad in the world that sent men to the moon. We boast the largest theme park facility in the United States, the origins of stock car racing, and we're pretty sure we have the only city hall ever imploded in the opening scenes of a Mel Gibson movie. We have the largest number of American bald eagles of any state in the lower 48, we produce more oranges for orange juice than any other region in North America, and we claim the busiest cruise port in the Western Hemisphere. Three very large creatures call Central Florida home: two that are quite nice—the manatee and the sea turtle—and one, not so nice— the alligator. All are quite amazing to see.

We turn one cliché right on its head: Orlando is a nice place to visit, and many of you *will* want to live here. And why not? How do you think we ended up becoming the fastest growing state in the United States, three years in a row?

ACKNOWLEDGMENTS

Many thanks to Fern Matthews and Erin L. Hefferan of the Orlando-UCF Shakespeare Festival; Leslie Sheffield and the Florida State Archives; Bob Kealing for his assistance with information on the Kerouac Project; Camille Dudley of Universal Orlando; Jacquelyn Wilson of SeaWorld; Dr. Tana M. Porter, Research Librarian, and Cynthia Cardona, Photo Conservationist of the OCRHC; Ray Ratto of the *San Francisco Chronicle*, for his review of the sports material; Dave Marsh of WESH T.V. for his help with the weather information; Dr. Carl "Sandy" Dann III who not only shared his stories with me and helped me find the cover postcard—he paid for lunch! Also thanks to Dean Padgett, The Winter Park Public Library History Archives; Sara Ann Harris, the Louisiana Seafood Board; Cindy Turner, Historic Bok Sanctuary; the wonderful and kind Gertrude F. Laframboise of Rollins College; Steve Rajtar for his willingness to let me use his research for the downtown Orlando tour; Bonnie Abellera of FF&WCC; Melanie Neland of ISC; Marge Bell of stillnature.com; Mrs. Peggy Strong; Bill Dreggors, Executive Director, the West Volusia Historical Society; my friend Lydia Gardner, Clerk of the Courts for Orange County who continued to urge me onward; my neighbors and friends Gene and Marianne Randall for help taking pictures on that cloudy Sunday; and to Mr. Russell V. Hughes who came to my rescue with wonderful vintage postcards.

I could not have completed this book without the editing expertise of Evelyn W. Pettit. A long-time professional editor, Ms. Pettit is now the owner of Brandywine Books in Winter Park, Florida, an antiquarian bookstore on Park Avenue. It is there I met Evelyn and her late husband Bill one day in 1989, when I dropped in to peruse their shelves. It was the beginning of a friendship that has lasted 14 years—and counting. Thanks Evelyn!

Thanks to: the Rollins College Department of Archives and Special Collections, Olin Library; the Orange County Regional History Center; Leu Gardens; the Florida Fish and Wildlife Conservation Commission; Historic Bok Sanctuary; SeaWorld Adventure Park; the Central Florida Zoo; Universal Orlando; Orlando-UCF Shakespeare Theater; Orlando Science Center; Maitland Art Center; Don Garlits Museum of Drag Racing; Orlando Museum of Art; the Mennello Museum of American Folk Art; Daytona International Speedway; NASA; the National Hurricane Center; the Florida State Photo Archives; Friends of the Marjorie Kinnan Rawlings Farm; Enzian Theater; West Volusia Historical Society; Phil Eschbach, and Jim Angy for supplying me with pictures, graphics, vintage postcards, and photos for use in this book.

BIBLIOGRAPHY

Bacon, Eve. *Orlando: A Centennial History* (2 vols.). Chuluota, FL: Mickler House, Publishers, 1975 (out of print).

Bigelow, Gordon E. *Frontier Eden: The Literary Career of Marjorie Kinnan Rawlings.* University Press of Florida, 1966 and 1989.

Blackman, William Fremont. *History of Orange County, Florida*. DeLand, FL: E. O. Painter, Printer, 1927; Chuluota, FL: Mickler House, Publishers, 1973 (out of print).

Brandon, Pam, ed. *Walt Disney World Resort: 100 Years of Magic Celebration* (media guide). Lake Buena Vista, FL: Walt Disney World Media Relations, 2000.

Chapman, Robin. Interview with Emily Bavar Kelly. Lake Buena Vista, FL: Archives, Walt Disney World Resort, 1996. Used in 25th-Anniversary video Robin Chapman produced for the Walt Disney World Resort in 1996. It ran at the Welcome Center in the Magic Kingdom.

Chapman, Robin. *The Absolutely Essential® Guide to Winter Park*. Winter Park, FL: Absolutely Essential Co., 2001.

Cheney, Judge Donald A. "The Dinky," Rollins Alumni *Record*, October 1967.

"Dugong," *Microsoft® Encarta® Online Encyclopedia*. 2002. http://encarta.msn.com.

Florida Grower Magazine. Special Edition on Citrus History. August 2000.

Fries, Kena. *Orlando in the Long, Long, Ago ... and Now*. Orlando: Tyn Cobb Florida Press, 1938 (out of print).

Fries, Otto. Letter to Kena Fries, 1873 (unpublished; available at the Orange County Regional History Center, Orlando, FL).

Jarvis, N. S. The Diary of Captain N. S. Jarvis, Army physician in Florida, 1837 (unpublished; available at the Orange County Regional History Center, Orlando, FL).

Jordan, E. L.; illustrations by Walter Ferguson and John Cody. *Hammond's Nature Atlas of America*. New York: C. S. Hammond and Co., 1952 (out of print).

Kelly, Emily Bavar. "Journalist Who Broke Disney Story Dies at 88," *Orlando Sentinel*, July 2003 (obituary).

Kleinberg, Eliot. *Florida Fun Facts*. Sarasota, FL: Pineapple Press, 1995.

"Manatee," *Microsoft® Encarta® Online Encyclopedia*. 2002. http://encarta.msn.com.

Morris, Allen. *Florida Place Names*. Coral Gables, FL: University of Miami Press, 1974; Sarasota, FL: Pineapple Press, 1995.

National Audubon Society Field Guide to Florida. New York: Alfred A. Knopf, 1998.

Peterson, Roger Tory. *A Field Guide to the Birds East of the Rockies*. Boston: Houghton Mifflin Co., 1980 (out of print).

Rawlings, Marjorie Kinnan. *Cross Creek*. New York: Charles Scribner's Sons, 1942.

Rawlings, Marjorie Kinnan. *The Yearling*. New York: Charles Scribner's Sons, 1938.

Robinson, Jim, and Andrews, Mark. *Flashbacks: The Story of Central Florida's Past*. Orlando, FL: Orange County Historical Society and the Orlando Sentinel, 1995 (out of print).

Smith, Margaret. *The Edward Bok Legacy: A History of Bok Tower Gardens*. Lake Wales, FL: Bok Tower Gardens Foundation, 2002.

What's Cookin' in Florida. Kansas City, MO: Bev-Ron Publishing Co., 1967 (out of print).

Williams, John M., and Duedall, Iver W. *Florida Hurricanes and Tropical Storms: 1871-2001*. Gainesville: University Press of Florida, 2002.

Winn, Ed. *The Early History of the St. Johns River*. Maitland, FL: Winn's Books, no date.

INDEX

ORLANDO NOTES

ORLANDO NOTES

ORLANDO NOTES

ORLANDO NOTES

ORLANDO NOTES

This book was designed by
Eileen Schechner
and printed by
Mercury Printers
Orlando, Florida
October 2003